Advance Praise for
Dumbing Us Down

Ever since winning notice as the New York State Teacher of the Year, John Taylor Gatto has been offered opportunities to share his critique of compulsory education. People from all across North America responded so strongly to his talks and occasional articles, that we asked him to write the longer pieces collected here in *Dumbing Us Down*. Here's some of what people are saying about John's work:

"Your words hit the nail on the head. Our schools leave no time for kids to be with parents and the community. The seeds of your ideas are here ready to sprout."
— Bonni McKeown, Capon Springs, WV

"I heard you speak on the McNeill/Lehrer News Hour and am in complete agreement with you. When I first started teaching here, I was amazed to find everything the same as in New York City—the same insane assumptions, the same insane beliefs, the same insane way of doing things, the same lack of education."
— Ed Rauchut, NEH Teacher/Scholar for Nebraska, Omaha, NE

"Your words very concisely captured all my frustrations and concerns of wanting to be an 'educator' in a society that schools well but fails to educate. Amen, Amen, Amen! is my response."
— Kathleen Trumbull, Teacher, Silver Bay, MN

"I am not an educator, nor a parent, nor a concerned citizen. I am a product of the problems you describe. Although I had a passionate desire to learn, some excellent teachers and a diploma, I realized very soon how almost useless the whole experience had been for

me. Parents, students, especially the students, need to know the things you talk about."
— Praya Desai, Philadelphia, PA

"Anyone like John Gatto, with the courage and tenacity to go against the bureaucratic hierarchy, is looked upon as a troublemaker. But the principles that John espouses are really not new or radical, but fundamental to learning anything. The fact that that they seem controversial to current administrators shows how far they have strayed from the real purpose of their employment."
— Ron Hitchon, Intermodal East, Secaucus, NJ

"Your analysis of the crisis in schooling, its difference from real education and the relation between schooling/television and the apathetic blindered world view so prevalent among Americans really gets to the root of our disintegrated society. "
— David Werner, The Hesperian Foundation, Palo Alto, CA

"What you say is really happening on my island. It is very true that schooling is made for those people who are intended to be controlled and their lives predicted."
— Alfred T. Apatang, Rota, M.P.

"You have enlightened as well as frightened me. I will think carefully about many many things but ever so carefully about bringing the human spirit back into my classroom to help my children see and feel the wholeness of their lives."
— Ruth Schmitt, Tuba City, AZ

"The highest compliment I can offer you as a teacher is to say I am impressed with your students."
— Bob Kerrey, Senator, NE

"I am thrilled by your analysis, recommendations and insight."
— Pat Farenga, John Holt Associates

DUMBING US DOWN

The Hidden Curriculum of Compulsory Schooling

John Taylor Gatto

New Society Publishers

Philadelphia, PA   Gabriola Island, BC

Library of Congress Cataloging-in-Publication Data

Gatto, John Taylor.
 Dumbing us down : the hidden curriculum of compulsory schooling /
 John Taylor Gatto. — Philadelphia: New Society Publishers, c1992.
  xiv, 104 p. ; 23 cm.
 includes bibliographical references.
 ISBN 0-86571-230-1. — ISBN 0-86571-231-X (pbk.)
  1. Gatto, John Taylor. 2. Educators—United States—Biography. 3.
Education—United States—Philosophy.   I. Title.
LA2317.G33A3 1992   92-198127

® GCIU ™

Inquiries regarding requests to reprint all or part of *Dumbing Us Down: The Hidden Curriculum of Compulsory Schooling* should be addressed to New Society Publishers, 4527 Springfield Avenue, Philadelphia, PA, 19143.

 ISBN Hardcover   USA 0-86571-230-1   CAN 1-55092-174-6
 ISBN Paperback   USA 0-86571-231-X   CAN 1-55092-175-4

Cover design by g.e. jarrett. Book design by Martin Kelley. Printed on partially-recycled paper using soy-based ink by Capital City Press of Montpelier, Vermont.

To order directly from the publisher, add $2.50 to the price for the first copy, and add 75¢ for each additional copy. Send check or money order to:
 In the United States: *In Canada:*
 New Society Publishers   New Society Publishers
 4527 Springfield Avenue   PO Box 189
 Philadelphia, PA 19143   Gabriola Island, BC VOR 1XO

New Society Publishers is a project of the New Society Educational Foundation, a nonprofit, tax-exempt, public foundation in the United States, and of the Catalyst Education Society, a nonprofit society in Canada. Opinions expressed in this book do not necessarily represent positions of the New Society Educational Foundation, nor the Catalyst Education Society.

Table of Contents

Biographical Note ix
The Seven-Lesson Schoolteacher 1
The Psychopathic School 23
The Green Monongahela 39
We Need Less School,
    Not More 51
The Congregational Principle 81

Dedication

I dedicate this book to my granddaughter, whose name in Icelandic means "the writing of God." Sparkle and shine in the face of darkness, Gvuthrune.

Publisher's Note

The social philosopher Hannah Arendt once wrote that, "The aim of totalitarian education has never been to instill convictions but to destroy the capacity to form any."*

If one were to poll our nation's leading educators about what the goal of our educational systems should be, I suspect one would come up with as many goals as educators. But I also imagine that the capacity to form one's own convictions independent of what was being taught in the classroom, the ability to think critically based upon one's own experience, would not rank high on many lists. In fact, the idea that the goal of education might have little to do with what goes on in the classroom would likely strike most educators, of whatever political stripe, as heresy.

In the context of our culture, it is easy to see that critical thinking is a threat. As parents, we all want what is "best" for our children. Yet, by our own actions and lifestyles, and through the demands that we place on our educational institutions, it is clear that by "best" we all-too-often mean "most." This shift from the qualitative to the quantitative, from thinking about what is best for the holistic development of the individual human being to thinking about which resources should be available to semi-monopoly governmental educational institutions certainly does not bear close scrutiny.

Shouldn't we also ask ourselves what the consequences are of scrambling to provide the "most" of everything to our children in a world of fast-dwindling resources? What does the mad and often brutally competitive scramble for resources—for more pay for teachers, for more equipment, for more money for schools—teach our children about us? More crucially, what message does this mad scramble send to those children who, through no fault of their own, lose out in the competition? And what would be the cost to the social fabric if our children's convictions were based on their experience? (Perhaps we are already paying the cost of the development of such convictions, however poorly articulated, in the forms of violence, chemical dependency, teenage pregnancy, and a host of other social ills affecting today's young people?)

Eclectic, engaging, and not readily pigeon-holed, John Taylor Gatto's thinking forces us to re-examine some of our most cherished assumptions in the light of his and his students' day-to-day experience. He provides few ready made solutions or optimistic answers for the future of our schools. What he does provide through the example of his twenty-six years of teaching is first a commitment to providing *quality* options to the poor and disadvantaged, who are most in need of them, and second conscienticization so that at least his students come to some critical understanding of what is being done to them in the name of "schooling."

Gatto's vision of our social order may be bleak, but it also provides at least a ray of hope in the example and idea that free-thinking and critically aware indviduals, freely united in newly reconstructed communities can correct social ills and lead us toward a future truly worth living in. Because we share the conviction that this is both desirable and possible, we at New Society Publishers are proud to publish *Dumbing Us Down.*

David H. Albert
for New Society Publishers
13 June 1991

*Hanna Arendt, *Totalitarianism* (New York: Harcourt Brace Jovanovich, 1968), p168.

BIOGRAPHICAL NOTE

I'm here to talk to you about ideas, but I think a purpose might be served in telling a little bit about myself so I become a person like you rather than just another talking head from the television set. I know that sometimes when I hear a news report from TV I wonder, Who are *you?* and, Why are you telling me these things? So let me offer you some of the ground of out of which these ideas grew.

I've worked as a New York City schoolteacher for the past twenty-six years, teaching for some of that time elite children from Manhattan's Upper West Side between Lincoln Center, where the opera is, and Columbia University, where the defense contracts are; and teaching, in most recent years, children from Harlem and Spanish Harlem, whose lives are shaped by the dangerous undercurrents of the industrial city in decay. I've taught at six different schools in that time. My present school is in the shadow of St. John the Divine Cathedral, the largest Gothic structure in the United States, and not a long walk from the famous Museum of Natural History and the Metropolitan Museum of Art. About three blocks from my school is the spot where the "Central Park jogger," (as media mythology refers to her) was raped and brutally beaten a few years ago; seven of the nine attackers went to school in my district.

My own perspective on things, however, was shaped a long way from New York City, in the river town of Monongahela, Pennsylvania, forty miles southeast of Pittsburgh. In those days, Monongahela was a place of steel mills and coal mines, of paddle-wheel river steamers churning the emerald green water chemical orange, of respect for hard work and family life. Monongahela was a place with muted class distinctions since everyone was more or less poor, although very few, I suspect, *knew* they were poor. It was a place where independence, toughness, and self-reliance were honored, a place where pride in ethnic and local culture was very intense. It was an altogether wonderful place to grow up, even to grow up poor. People talked to each other, minding each other's business, instead of the abstract business of "the world." Indeed, the larger world hardly extended beyond Pittsburgh, a wonderful, dark, steel city worth a trip to see once or twice a year. Nobody in my memory felt confined by Monongahela or dwelled, within my earshot, on the possibility they were missing something important by not being elsewhere.

My grandfather was the town printer and had been for a time the publisher of the town newspaper, *The Daily Republican*—a name which attracted some attention because the town was a stronghold of the Democratic party. From my grandfather and his independent

German ways I learned a great deal that I might have missed if I had grown up in a time, like today, when old people are put away in a home or kept out of sight.

Living in Manhattan has been for me in many ways like living on the moon. Even though I've been here for thirty-five years, my heart and habit are still in Monongahela. Nevertheless, the shock of Manhattan's very different society and values sharpened my sense of difference and made me an anthropologist as well as a schoolteacher. Over the past twenty-six years, I've used my classes as a laboratory where *I* could learn a broader range of what human possibility is—the whole catalogue of hopes and fears—and also as a place where I could study what releases and what inhibits human power. During that time, I've come to believe that genius is an exceedingly common human quality, probably natural to most of us. I didn't want to accept that notion—far from it—my own training in two elite universities taught me that intelligence and talent distributed themselves economically over a bell curve and that human destiny, because of those mathematical, seemingly irrefutable, scientific facts, was as rigorously determined as John Calvin contended. The trouble was that the unlikeliest kids kept demonstrating to me at random moments so many of the hallmarks of human excellence—insight, wisdom, justice, resourcefulness, courage, originality—that I became confused. They didn't do this often enough to make my teaching easy, but they did it often enough that I began to wonder, reluctantly, whether it was possible that being in school itself was what was dumbing them down. Was it possible I had been hired not to enlarge children's power, but to diminish it? That seemed crazy on the face of it, but slowly I began to realize that the bells and the confinement, the crazy sequences, the age-segregation, the lack of privacy, the constant surveillance, and all the rest of the national curriculum of schooling were designed exactly as if someone had set out to *prevent* children from learning how to think and act, to coax them into addiction and dependent behavior.

Bit by bit I began to devise guerrilla exercises to allow the kids I taught—as many as I was able—the raw material people have always used to educate themselves: privacy, choice, freedom from surveillance, and as broad a range of situations and human associations as my limited power and resources could manage. In simpler terms, I tried to maneuver them into positions where they would have a chance to be their own teachers and to make themselves the major text of their own education.

In theoretical, metaphorical terms, the idea I began to explore was this one: that teaching is nothing like the art of painting, where, by the *addition* of material to a surface, an image is synthetically produced, but more like the art of sculpture, where, by the *subtraction* of material, an image already locked in the stone is enabled to emerge. It is a crucial distinction.

In other words, I dropped the idea that I was an expert, whose job it was to fill the little heads with my expertise, and began to explore how I could remove those obstacles that prevented the inherent genius of children from gathering itself. I no longer felt comfortable defining my work as bestowing wisdom on a struggling classroom audience. Although I continue to this day in those futile assays because of the nature of institutional teaching, wherever possible I have broken with teaching tradition and sent kids down their separate paths to their own private truths.

The sociology of government monopoly schools has evolved in such a way that a premise like mine jeopardizes the total institution if it spreads. Kept contained, the occasional teacher who makes a discovery like mine is at worst an annoyance to the chain of command (which has evolved automatic defenses to isolate such bacilli and then neutralize or destroy them.) But once loose the idea could imperil the central assumptions which allow the institutional school to sustain itself, such as the false assumption that it is difficult to learn to read, or that kids resist learning, and many more. Indeed, the very stability of our economy is threatened by any form of education that might change the nature of the human product schools now turn out; the economy schoolchildren currently expect to live under and serve would not survive a generation of young people trained, for example, to think critically.

Success in my practice involves a large component of automatic trust, categorical trust, not the kind conditional on performance. People have to be allowed to make their own mistakes and try again, or they will never *master* themselves, although they may well *seem* to be competent when they have in fact only memorized or imitated someone else's performance. Success in my practice also involves a challenging of many comfortable assumptions about what is worth learning and out of what material a good life is fashioned.

Over the years of wrestling with the obstacles that stand between child and education I have come to believe that government monopoly schools are structurally unreformable. They cannot function if their central myths are exposed and abandoned. Over the years, I have come to see that whatever I thought I was doing as a teacher, most of what I actually was doing was teaching an invisible curriculum that reinforced the myths of the school institution and those of an economy based on caste. When I was trying to decide what to say to you that might make my experience as a schoolteacher useful, it occurred to me that I could best serve by telling you what I do that is wrong, rather than what I do that is right. What I do that is right is simple to understand—I get out of kids' way, I give them space and time and respect. What I do that is wrong, however, is strange, complex, and frightening. Let me begin to show you what that is.

A BRIEF NOTE ON FAMILY

Since I refer frequently to the family in the essays that follow, I want to make it clear that in my view each of us decides what "family" means in the arena of his of her heart. So far as I am concerned, no authority may presume to impose a centralized definition, a well-regulated orthodoxy, on the varied and vital entities that can be called "family."

THE SEVEN-LESSON
SCHOOLTEACHER

I

Call me Mr. Gatto, please. Twenty-six years ago, having nothing better to do with myself at the time, I tried my hand at schoolteaching. The license I have certifies that I am an instructor of English language and English literature, but that isn't what I do at all. I don't teach English, I teach school—and I win awards doing it.

Teaching means different things in different places, but seven lessons are universally taught from Harlem to Hollywood Hills. They constitute a national curriculum you pay for in more ways than you can imagine, so you might as well know what it is. You are at liberty, of course, to regard these lessons any way you like, but believe me when I say I intend no irony in this presentation. These are the things I

This speech was given on the occasion of the the author being named "New York State Teacher of the Year" for 1991.

teach, these are the things you pay me to teach. Make of them what you will.

1. CONFUSION

A lady named Kathy wrote this to me from Dubois, Indiana the other day:

> What big ideas are important to little kids? Well, the the biggest idea I think they need is that what they are learning isn't idiosyncratic—that there is some system to it all and it's not just raining down on them as they helplessly absorb. That's the task, to understand, to make coherent.

Kathy has it wrong. *The first lesson I teach is confusion. Everything* I teach is out of context. I teach the un-relating of everything. I teach dis-connections. I teach too much: the orbiting of planets, the law of large numbers, slavery, adjectives, architectural drawing, dance, gymnasium, choral singing, assemblies, surprise guests, fire drills, computer languages, parents' nights, staff-development days, pull-out programs, guidance with strangers my students may never see again, standardized tests, age-segregation unlike anything seen in the outside world....What do any of these things have to do with each other?

Even in the best schools a close examination of curriculum and its sequences turns up a lack of coherence, full of internal contradictions. Fortunately the children have no words to define the panic and anger they feel *at constant violations of natural order and sequence* fobbed off on them as quality in education. The logic of the school-mind is that it is better to leave school with a tool kit of superficial jargon derived from economics, sociology, natural science, and so on, than with one genuine enthusiasm. But quality in education entails learning about something in depth. Confusion is thrust upon kids by too many strange adults, each working alone with only the thinnest relationship with each other, pretending, for the most part, to an expertise they do not possess.

Meaning, not disconnected facts, is what sane human beings seek, and education is a set of codes for processing raw data into meaning. Behind the patchwork quilt of school sequences and the school obsession with facts and theories, the age-old human search for meaning lies well concealed. This is harder to see in elementary school where the hierarchy of school experience seems to make better sense because the good-natured simple relationship between "let's do this" and "let's do that "is just assumed to mean something and the clientele has not yet consciously discerned how little substance is behind the play and pretense.

Think of the great natural sequences —like learning to walk and learning to talk; the progression of light from sunrise to sunset; the ancient procedures of a farmer, a smithy, or a shoemaker; or the preparation of a Thanksgiving feast—all of the parts are in perfect harmony with each other, each action justifies itself and illuminates the past and the future. School sequences aren't like that, not inside a single class and not among the total menu of daily classes. School sequences are crazy. There is no particular reason for any of them, nothing that bears close scrutiny. Few teachers would dare to teach the tools whereby dogmas of a school or a teacher could be criticized, since everything must be accepted. School subjects are learned, if they *can* be learned, like children learn the catechism or memorize the Thirty-nine Articles of Anglicanism.

I teach the un-relating of everything, an infinite fragmentation the opposite of cohesion; what I do is more related to television programming than to making a scheme of order. In a world where home is only a ghost, because both parents work, or because of too many moves or too many job changes or too much ambition, or because something else has left everybody too confused to maintain a family relation, I teach you how to accept confusion as your destiny. That's the first lesson I teach.

2. CLASS POSITION

The second lesson I teach is class position. I teach that students must stay in the class where they belong. I don't know who decides my kids belong there but that's not my business. The children are numbered so that if any get away they can be returned to the right class. Over the years the variety of ways children are numbered by schools has increased dramatically, until it is hard to see the human beings plainly under the weight of numbers they carry. Numbering children is a big and very profitable undertaking, though what the strategy is designed to accomplish is elusive. I don't even know why parents would, without a fight, allow it to be done to their kids.

In any case, that's not my business. My job is to make them like being locked together with children who bear numbers like their own. Or at the least to endure it like good sports. If I do my job well, the kids can't even *imagine* themselves somewhere else, because I've shown them how to envy and fear the better classes and how to have contempt for the dumb classes. Under this efficient discipline the class mostly polices itself into good marching order. That's the real lesson of any rigged competition like school. You come to know your place.

In spite of the overall class blueprint, which assumes that ninety-nine percent of the kids are in their class to stay, I nevertheless make a public effort to exhort children to higher levels of test success, hinting at eventual transfer from the lower class as a reward. I frequently insinuate the day will come when an employer will hire them on the basis of test scores and grades, even though my own experience is that employers are rightly indifferent to such things. I never lie outright, but I've come to see that truth and schoolteaching are, at bottom, incompatible, just as Socrates said thousands of years ago. The lesson of numbered classes is that everyone has a proper place in the pyramid and there is no way out of your class except by number magic. Failing that, you must stay where you are put.

3. INDIFFERENCE

The third lesson I teach is indifference. I teach children not to care too much about anything, even though they want to make it appear that they do. How I do this is very subtle. I do it by demanding that they become totally involved in my lessons, jumping up and down in their seats with anticipation, competing vigorously with each other for my favor. It's heartwarming when they do that; it impresses everyone, even me. When I'm at my best I plan lessons very carefully in order to produce this show of enthusiasm. But when the bell rings I insist they drop whatever it is we have been doing and proceed quickly to the next work station. They must turn on and off like a light switch. Nothing important is ever finished in my class nor in any class I know of. Students never have a complete experience except on the installment plan.

Indeed, the lesson of bells is that no work is worth finishing, so why care too deeply about anything? Years of bells will condition all but the strongest to a world that can no longer offer important work to do. Bells are the secret logic of schooltime; their logic is inexorable. Bells destroy the past and future, rendering every interval the same as any other, as the abstraction of a map renders every living mountain and river the same, even though they are not. Bells inoculate each undertaking with indifference.

4. EMOTIONAL DEPENDENCY

The fourth lesson I teach is emotional dependency. By stars and red checks, smiles and frowns, prizes, honors, and disgraces, I teach kids to surrender their will to the predestinated chain of command. Rights may be granted or withheld by any authority without appeal, because rights do not exist inside a school— not even the right of free speech, as the Supreme Court has ruled— unless school authorities say they do. As a schoolteacher, I intervene in many personal decisions, issuing a pass for those I deem legitimate, or initiating a disciplinary confrontation for behavior that threatens my control. Individuality is constantly trying to assert itself among children and teenagers, so my judgments come thick and fast. Individuality is a contradiction of class theory, a curse to all systems of classification.

Here are some common ways it shows up: children sneak away for a private moment in the toilet on the pretext of moving their bowels, or they steal a private instant in the hallway on the grounds they need water. I know they don't, but I allow them to "deceive" me because this conditions them to depend on my favors. Sometimes free will appears right in front of me in pockets of children angry, depressed, or happy about things outside my ken; rights in such matters cannot be recognized by schoolteachers, only privileges that can be withdrawn, hostages to good behavior.

5. INTELLECTUAL DEPENDENCY

The fifth lesson I teach is intellectual dependency. Good students wait for a teacher to tell them what to do. It is the most important lesson, that we must wait for other people, better trained than ourselves, to make the meanings of our lives. The expert makes all the important choices; only I, the teacher, can determine what my kids must study, or rather, only the people who pay me can make those decisions, which I then enforce. If I'm told that evolution is a fact instead of a theory, I transmit that as ordered, punishing deviants who resist what I have been told to tell them to think. This power to control what children will think lets me separate successful students from failures very easily.

Successful children do the thinking I assign them with a minimum of resistance and a decent show of enthusiasm. Of the millions of things of value to study, I decide what few we have time for, or actually it is decided by my faceless employers. The choices are theirs, why should I argue? Curiosity has no important place in my work, only conformity.

Bad kids fight this, of course, even though they lack the concepts to know what they are fighting, struggling to make decisions for themselves about what they will learn and when they will learn it. How can we allow that and survive as schoolteachers? Fortunately there are tested procedures to break the will of those who resist; it is more difficult, naturally, if the kids have respectable parents who come to their aid, but that happens less and less in spite of the bad reputation of schools. No middle-class parents I have ever met actually believe that *their* kid's school is one of the bad ones. Not one single parent in twenty-six years of teaching. That's amazing, and probably the best testimony to what happens to families when mother and father have been well-schooled themselves, learning the seven lessons.

Good people wait for an expert to tell them what to do. It is hardly an exaggeration to say that our entire economy depends upon this lesson being learned. Think of what might fall apart if children weren't trained to be dependent: the social services could hardly survive; they would vanish, I think, into the recent historical limbo out of which they arose. Counselors and therapists would look on in horror as the supply of psychic invalids vanished. Commercial entertainment of all sorts, including television, would wither as people learned again how to make their own fun. Restaurants, the prepared-food industry, and a whole host of other assorted food services would be drastically down-sized if people returned to making their own meals rather than depending on strangers to plant, pick, chop, and cook for them. Much of modern law, medicine, and engineering would go too, the clothing business and schoolteaching as well, unless a guaranteed supply of helpless people continued to pour out of our schools each year.

Don't be too quick to vote for radical school reform if you want to continue getting a paycheck. We've built a way of life that depends on people doing what they are told because they don't know how to tell *themselves* what to do. It's one of the biggest lessons I teach.

6. PROVISIONAL SELF-ESTEEM

The sixth lesson I teach is provisional self-esteem. If you've ever tried to wrestle into line kids whose parents have convinced them to believe they'll be loved in spite of anything, you know how impossible it is to make self-confident spirits conform. Our world wouldn't survive a flood of confident people very long, so I teach that a kid's self-respect should depend on expert opinion. My kids are constantly evaluated and judged.

A monthly report, impressive in its provision, is sent into a student's home to elicit approval or mark exactly, down to a single percentage point, how dissatisfied with the child a parent should be. The ecology of "good" schooling depends on perpetuating dissatisfaction, just as the commercial economy depends on the same fertilizer. Although some people might be surprised how little time or reflection goes into making up these mathematical records, the cumulative weight of these objective-seeming documents establishes a profile that compels children to arrive at certain decisions about themselves and their futures based on the casual judgment of strangers. Self-evaluation, the staple of every major philosophical system that ever appeared on the planet, is never considered a factor. The lesson of report cards, grades, and tests is that children should not trust themselves or their parents but should instead rely on the evaluation of certified officials. People need to be told what they are worth.

7. ONE CAN'T HIDE

The seventh lesson I teach is that one can't hide. I teach students they are always watched, that each is under constant surveillance by myself and my colleagues. There are no private spaces for children, there is no private time. Class change lasts exactly three hundred seconds to keep promiscuous fraternization at low levels. Students are encouraged to tattle on each other or even to tattle on their own parents. Of course, I encourage parents to file reports about their own child's waywardness too. A family trained to snitch on itsef isn't likely to conceal any dangerous secrets.

I assign a type of extended schooling called "homework," so that the effect of surveillance, if not that surveillance itself, travels into private households, where students might otherwise use free time to learn something unauthorized from a father or mother, by exploration, or by apprenticing to some wise person in the neighborhood. Disloyalty to the idea of schooling is a devil always ready to find work for idle hands.

The meaning of constant surveillance and denial of privacy is that no one can be trusted, that privacy is not legitimate. Surveillance is an ancient imperative, espoused by certain influential thinkers, a central prescription set down in *The Republic*, in *The City of God*, in the *Institutes of the Christian Religion*, in *New Atlantis*, in *Leviathan*, and in a host of other places. All these childless men who wrote these books discovered the same thing: children must be closely watched if you want to keep a society under tight central control. Children will follow a private drummer if you can't get them into a uniformed marching band.

II

It is the great triumph of compulsory government monopoly mass-schooling that among even the best of my fellow teachers, and among even the best of my students' parents, only a small number can imagine a different way to do things. "The kids have to know how to read and write, don't they?" "They have to know how to add and subtract, don't they?" "They have to learn to follow orders if they ever expect to keep a job."

Only a few lifetimes ago things were very different in the United States. Originality and variety were common currency; our freedom from regimentation made us the miracle of the world; social-class boundaries were relatively easy to cross; our citizenry was marvelously confident, inventive, and able to do much for themselves independently, and to think for themselves. We were something special, we Americans, all by ourselves, without government sticking its nose into and measuring every aspect of our lives, without institutions and social agencies telling us how to think and feel. We were something special, as individuals, as Americans.

But we've had a society essentially under central control in the United States since just before the Civil War, and such a society requires compulsory schooling, government monopoly schooling, to maintain itself. Before this development schooling wasn't very important anywhere. We had it, but not too much of it, and only as much as an individual *wanted*. People learned to read, write, and do arithmetic just fine anyway; there are some studies that suggest literacy at the time of the American Revolution, at least for non-slaves on the Eastern seaboard, was close to total. Thomas Paine's *Common Sense* sold 600,000 copies to a population of 3,000,000, twenty percent of whom were slaves, and fifty percent indentured servants.

Were the colonists geniuses? No, the truth is that reading, writing, and arithmetic only take about one hundred hours to transmit as long as the audience is eager and willing to learn. The trick is to wait until someone asks and then move fast while the mood is on. Millions of people teach themselves these things, it really isn't very hard. Pick up a fifth-grade math or rhetoric textbook from 1850 and you'll see that the texts were pitched then on what would today be considered college level. The continuing cry for "basic skills" practice is a smoke screen behind which schools preempt the time of children for twelve years and teach them the seven lessons I've just described to you.

The society that has come increasingly under central control since just before the Civil War shows itself in the lives we lead, the clothes we wear, the food we eat, and the green highway signs we drive by from coast to coast, all of which are the products of this control. So too, I think, are the epidemics of drugs, suicide, divorce, violence, cruelty, and hardening of class into caste in the United States products of the dehumanization of our lives, the lessening of individual, family, and community importance, a diminishment that proceeds from central control. The character of large compulsory institutions is inevitable; they want more and more until there isn't any more to give. School takes our children away from any possibility of an active role in community life—in fact it destroys communities by relegating the training of children to the hands of certified experts—and by doing so it ensures our children cannot grow up fully human. Aristotle taught that without a fully active role in community life one could not hope to become a healthy human being. Surely he was right. Look around you the next time you are near a school or an old people's reservation if you wish a demonstration.

School as it was built is an essential support system for a model of social engineering that condemns most people to be subordinate stones in a pyramid that narrows as it ascends to a terminal of control. School is an artifice that makes such a pyramidical social order seem inevitable, although such a premise is a fundamental betrayal of the American Revolution. From Colonial days through the period of the Republic we had no schools to speak of—read Benjamin Franklin's *Autobiography* for an example of a man who had no time to waste in school—and yet the promise of democracy was beginning to be realized. We turned our backs on this promise by bringing to life the ancient pharaonic dream of Egypt: compulsory subordination for all. That was the secret Plato reluctantly transmitted in *The Republic* when Glaucon and Adeimantus extort from Socrates the plan for total state control of human life, a plan necessary to maintain a society where some people take more than their share. "'I will show you," says Socrates, "'how to bring about such a feverish city, but you will not like what I am going to say." And so the blueprint of the seven-lesson school was first sketched.

The current debate about whether we should have a national curriculum is phony. We already have a national curriculum locked up in the seven lessons I have just outlined. Such a curriculum produces physical, moral, and intellectual paralysis, and no curriculum of content will be sufficient to reverse its hideous effects. What is currently under discussion in our national hysteria about failing academic performance misses the point. Schools teach exactly what they are intended to teach and they do it well: how to be a good Egyptian and remain in your place in the pyramid.

III

None of this is inevitable. None of it is impossible to overthrow. We do have choices in how we bring up young people; there is no one right way. If we broke through the power of the pyramidical illusion we would see that. There is no life-and-death international competition threatening our national existence, difficult as that idea is even to think about, let alone believe, in the face of a continual media barrage of myth to the contrary. In every important material respect our nation is self-sufficient, including in energy. I realize that idea runs counter to the most fashionable thinking of political economists, but the "profound transformation" of our economy these people talk about is neither inevitable nor irreversible. Global economics does not speak to the public need for meaningful work, affordable housing, fulfilling education, adequate medical care, a clean environment, honest and accountable government, social and cultural renewal, or simple justice. All global ambitions are based on a definition of productivity and the good life so alienated from common human reality I am convinced it is wrong and that most people would agree with me if they could perceive an alternative. We might be able to see that if we regained a hold on a philosophy that locates meaning where meaning is genuinely to be found—in families, in friends, in the passage of seasons, in nature, in simple ceremonies and rituals, in curiosity, generosity, compassion, and service to others, in a decent independence and privacy, in all the free and inexpensive things out of which real families, real friends, and real communities are built— then we would be so self-sufficient we would not even need the material "sufficiency" which our global "experts" are so insistent we be concerned about.

How did these awful places, these "schools" come about? Well, casual schooling has always been with us in a variety of forms, a mildly useful adjunct to growing up. But "modern schooling" as we now know it is a by-product of the two "Red Scares" of 1848 and 1919, when powerful interests feared a revolution among our own industrial poor. Partly, too, total schooling came about because old-line "American" families were appalled by the native cultures of Celtic, Slavic, and Latin immigrants of the 1840s and felt repugnance toward the Catholic religion they brought with them. Certainly a third contributing factor in creating a jail for children called school must have been the consternation with which these same "Americans" regarded the movement of African-Americans through the society in the wake of the Civil War.

Look again at the seven lessons of school-teaching—confusion, class position, indifference, emotional and intellectual dependency, conditional self-esteem, surveillance—all of these lessons are prime training for permanent underclasses, people deprived forever of finding the center of their own special genius. And over time this training has shaken loose from its own original logic: to regulate the poor. For since the 1920s the growth of the school bureaucracy, and the less visible growth of a horde of industries that profit from schooling exactly as it is, has enlarged this institution's original grasp to the point that it now seizes the sons and daughters of the middle classes as well.

Is it any wonder Socrates was outraged at the accusation he took money to teach? Even then, philosophers saw clearly the inevitable direction the professionalization of teaching would take, preempting the teaching function, which belongs to everyone in a healthy community.

With lessons like the ones I teach day after day it should be little wonder we have a real national crisis, the nature of which is very different from that proclaimed by the national media. Young people are indifferent to the adult world and to the future, indifferent to almost everything except the diversion of toys and violence. Rich or poor, school children who face the twenty-first century cannot concentrate on anything for very long; they have a poor sense of time past and time to come. They are mistrustful of intimacy like the children of divorce they really are (for we have divorced them from significant parental attention); they hate solitude, are cruel, materialistic, dependent, passive, violent, timid in the face of the unexpected, addicted to distraction.

All the peripheral tendencies of childhood are nourished and magnified to a grotesque extent by schooling, which, through its hidden curriculum, prevents effective personality development. Indeed, without exploiting the fearfulness, selfishness, and inexperience of children, our schools could not survive at all, nor could I as a certified schoolteacher. No common school that actually dared to teach the use of critical thinking tools—like the dialectic, the heuristic, or other devices that free minds should employ—would last very long before being torn to pieces. School has become the replacement for church in our secular society, and like church it requires that its teachings must be taken on faith.

It is time that we squarely face the fact that institutional schoolteaching is destructive to children. Nobody survives the *seven-lesson curriculum* completely unscathed, not even the instructors. The method is deeply and profoundly anti-educational. No tinkering will fix it. In one of the great ironies of human affairs, the massive rethinking the schools require would cost so much *less* than we are spending now that powerful interests cannot afford to let it happen. You must understand that first and foremost the business I am in is a *jobs project* and an agency for letting contracts. We cannot afford to save money by reducing the scope of our operation or by diversifying the product we offer, even to help children grow up right. That is the *iron law* of institutional schooling—it is a business, subject neither to normal accounting procedures nor to the rational scalpel of competition.

Some form of free-market system in public schooling is the likeliest place to look for answers, a free market where family schools and small entrepreneurial schools and religious schools and crafts schools and farm schools exist in profusion to compete with government education. I'm trying to describe a free market in schooling exactly like the one the country had until the Civil War, *one in which students volunteer for the kind of education that suits them*, even if that means self-education; it didn't hurt Benjamin Franklin that I can see. These options exist now in miniature, wonderful survivals of a strong and vigorous past, but they are available only to the resourceful, the courageous, the lucky, or the rich. The near impossibility of one of these better roads opening for the shattered families of the poor or for the bewildered host camped on the fringes of the urban middle class suggests that the disaster of *seven-lesson schools is going to grow unless we do something bold and decisive with the mess of government monopoly schooling.*

After an adult lifetime spent teaching school, I believe the *method* of mass-schooling is its only real content. Don't be fooled into thinking that good curriculum or good equipment or good teachers are the critical determinants of your son's or daughter's education. All the pathologies we've considered come about in large measure because the lessons of school prevent children keeping important appointments with themselves and with their families to learn lessons in self-motivation, perseverance, self-reliance, courage, dignity, and love—and lessons in service to others, too, which are among the key lessons of home and community life.

Thirty years ago these lessons could still be learned in the time left *after* school. But television has eaten up most of that time, and a combination of television and the stresses peculiar to two-income or single-parent families has swallowed up most of what used to be family time as well. Our kids have no time left to grow up fully human and only thin-soil wastelands to do it in.

A future is rushing down upon our culture that will insist all of us learn the wisdom of nonmaterial experience; a future that will demand as the price of survival that we follow a path of natural life economical in material cost. These lessons cannot be learned in schools as they are. School is a twelve-year jail sentence where bad habits are the only curriculum truly learned. I teach school and win awards doing it. I should know.

THE PSYCHOPATHIC SCHOOL

I accept this award on behalf of all the fine teachers I've known over the years who've struggled to make their transactions with children honorable ones, men and women who were never complacent, always questioning, always wrestling to define and redefine what the word "education" should mean. A Teacher of the Year is not the best teacher around (those people are too quiet to be easily uncovered), but she or he is a standard-bearer, representative of these private people who spend their lives gladly in the service of children. This is their award as well as mine.

1.

We live in a time of great school crisis linked to an even greater social crisis. Our nation ranks at the bottom of nineteen industrial nations in reading, writing, and arithmetic. At

---

This speech was given by the author on 31 January 1990 in accepting an award from the New York State Senate naming him New York City Teacher of the Year.

the very bottom. The world's narcotic economy is based upon our consumption of this commodity; if we didn't buy so many powdered dreams the business would collapse—and schools are an important sales outlet. Our teenage suicide rate is the highest in the world, and suicidal kids are rich kids for the most part, not the poor. In Manhattan, seventy percent of all new marriages last less than five years. So something is wrong for sure.

This great crisis which we witness in our schools is interlinked with a greater social crisis in the community. We seem to have lost our identity. Children and old people are penned up and locked away from the business of the world to a degree without precedent; nobody talks to them anymore, and without children and old people mixing in daily life; a community has no future and no past, only a continuous present. In fact the name "community" hardly applies to the way we interact with each other. We live in networks, not communities, and everyone I know is lonely because of that. School is a major actor in this tragedy, as it is a major actor in the widening gulf among social classes. Using school as a sorting mechanism, we appear to be on the way to creating a caste system, complete with untouchables who wander through subway trains begging and who sleep upon the streets.

I've noticed a fascinating phenomenon in my twenty-five years of teaching: that schools and schooling are increasingly irrelevant to the great enterprises of the planet. No one believes anymore that scientists are trained in science classes or politicians in civics classes or poets in English classes. The truth is that schools don't really teach anything except how to obey orders. This is a great mystery to me because thousands of humane, caring people work in schools, as teachers and aides and administrators, but the abstract logic of the institution overwhelms their individual contributions. Although teachers do care and do work very, very hard, the institution is psychopathic; it has no conscience. It rings a bell and the young man in the middle of writing a poem must close his notebook and move to a different cell where he must memorize that humans and monkeys derive from a common ancestor.

2.

Our form of compulsory schooling is an invention of the State of Massachusetts around 1850. It was resisted—sometimes with guns—by an estimated eighty percent of the Massachusetts population, the last outpost in Barnstable on Cape Cod not surrendering its children until the 1880s, when the area was seized by militia and children marched to school under guard.

Now here is a curious idea to ponder. Senator Ted Kennedy's office released a paper not too long ago claiming that *prior* to compulsory education the state literacy rate was ninety-eight percent, and after it the figure never exceeded ninety-one percent, where it stands in 1990.

Here is another curiosity to think about. The home-schooling movement has quietly grown to a size where one and half million young people are being educated entirely by their own parents; last month the education press reported the amazing news that children schooled at home seem to be five or even ten years ahead of their formally trained peers in their ability to think.

3.

I don't think we'll get rid of schools any time soon, certainly not in my lifetime, but if we're going to change what's rapidly becoming a disaster of ignorance, we need to realize that the school institution "schools" very well, though it does not "educate;" that's inherent in the design of the thing. It's not the fault of bad teachers or too little money spent. It's just impossible for education and schooling ever to be the same thing.

Schools were designed by Horace Mann and by Sears and Harper of the University of Chicago and by Thorndyke of Columbia Teachers College and by some other men to be instruments of the scientific management of a mass population. Schools are intended to produce, through the application of formulas, formulaic human beings whose behavior can be predicted and controlled.

To a very great extent schools succeed in doing this, but in a national order increasingly disintegrated, in a national order in which the only "successful" people are independent, self-reliant, confident, and individualistic (because community life which protects the dependent and the weak is dead and only networks remain), the products of schooling are, as I've said, irrelevant. Well-schooled people are irrelevant. They can sell film and razor blades, push paper and talk on telephones, or sit mindlessly before a flickering computer terminal, but as human beings they are useless. Useless to others and useless to themselves.

The daily misery around us is, I think, in large measure caused by the fact that, as Paul Goodman put it thirty years ago, we force children to grow up absurd. Any reform in schooling has to deal with its absurdities.

It is absurd and anti-life to be part of a system that compels you to sit in confinement with people of exactly the same age and social class. That system effectively cuts you off from the immense diversity of life and the synergy of variety; indeed it cuts you off from your own past and future, sealing you in a continuous present much the same way television does.

It is absurd and anti-life to move from cell to cell at the sound of a gong for every day of your natural youth in an institution that allows you no privacy and even follows you into the sanctuary of your home demanding that you do its "homework."

"How will they learn to read?" you ask, and
my answer is "Remember the lessons of
Massachusetts." When children are given
whole lives instead of age-graded ones in
cellblocks they learn to read, write, and do
arithmetic with ease, if those things make
sense in the kind of life that unfolds around
them.

But keep in mind that in the United States
almost nobody who reads, writes, or does
arithmetic gets much respect. We are a land of
talkers; we pay talkers the most and admire
talkers the most and so our children talk
constantly, following the public models of
television and schoolteachers. It is very difficult
to teach the "basics" anymore because they
really aren't basic to the society we've made.

4.

Two institutions at present control our
children's lives: television and schooling, in
that order. Both of these reduce the real world
of wisdom, fortitude, temperance, and justice
to a never-ending, nonstop abstraction. In
centuries past, the time of childhood and
adolescence would have been occupied in real
work, real charity, real adventures, and the
realistic search for mentors who might teach
what you really wanted to learn. A great deal
of time was spent in community pursuits,
practicing affection, meeting and studying
every level of the community, learning how to

make a home, and dozens of other tasks necessary to becoming a whole man or woman.

But here is the calculus of time the children I teach must deal with:

Out of the 168 hours in each week my children sleep 56. That leaves them 112 hours a week out of which to fashion a self.

According to recent reports children watch 55 hours of television a week. That then leaves them 57 hours a week in which to grow up.

My children attend school 30 hours a week, use about 8 hours getting ready for and traveling to and from school, and spend an average of 7 hours a week in homework—a total of 45 hours. During that time they are under constant surveillance. They have no private time or private space and are disciplined if they try to assert individuality in the use of time or space. That leaves them 12 hours a week out of which to create a unique consciousness. Of course my kids eat, too, and that takes some time—not much because they've lost the tradition of family dining—but if we allot 3 hours a week to evening meals we arrive at a net amount of private time for each child of 9 hours per week.

It's not enough, is it? The richer the kid, of course, the less television he or she watches, but the rich kid's time is just as narrowly prescribed by a somewhat broader catalogue of commercial entertainments and the inevitable assignment to a series of private lessons in areas seldom of his or her own choice.

But these activities are just a more cosmetic way to create dependent human beings, unable to fill their own hours, unable to initiate lines of meaning to give substance and pleasure to their existence. It's a national disease, this dependency and aimlessness, and I think schooling and television and lessons have a lot to do with it.

Think of the phenomena which are killing us as a nation—narcotic drugs, brainless competition, recreational sex, the pornography of violence, gambling, and alcohol, and the worst pornography of all: lives devoted to buying things, accumulation as a philosophy— all of these are addictions of dependent personalities, and this is what our brand of schooling must inevitably produce.

5.

I want to tell you what the effect on our children is of taking all their time from them—time they need to grow up—and forcing them to spend it on abstractions. You need to hear this because any reform that doesn't attack these specific pathologies will be nothing more than a facade.

1. The children I teach are indifferent to the adult world. This defies the experience of thousands of years. A close study of what big people were up to was always the most exciting occupation of youth, but nobody wants children to grow up these days, least of all the children; and who can blame them? *Toys are us.*

2. The children I teach have almost no curiosity, and what little they do have is transitory. They cannot concentrate for very long, even on things they choose to do. Can you see a connection between the bells ringing again and again to change classes and this phenomenon of evanescent attention?

3. The children I teach have a poor sense of the future, of how tomorrow is inextricably linked to today. As I said before, they live in a continuous present, the exact moment they are in is the boundary of their consciousness.

4. The children I teach are ahistorical; they have no sense of how the past has predestinated their own present, limiting their choices, shaping their values and lives.

5. The children I teach are cruel to each other; they lack compassion for misfortune; they laugh at weakness; they have contempt for people whose need for help shows too plainly.

6. The children I teach are uneasy with intimacy or candor. They cannot deal with genuine intimacy because of a lifelong habit of preserving a secret inner self inside a larger outer personality made up of artificial bits and pieces of behavior borrowed from television or acquired to manipulate teachers. Because they are not who they represent themselves to be, the disguise wears thin in the presence of intimacy; so intimate relationships have to be avoided.

7. The children I teach are materialistic, following the lead of schoolteachers who

materialistically "grade everything" and television mentors who offer everything in the world for sale.

8. The children I teach are dependent, passive, and timid in the presence of new challenges. This timidity is frequently masked by surface bravado, or by anger or aggressiveness, but underneath is a vacuum without fortitude.

I could name a few other conditions that school reform will have to tackle if our national decline is to be arrested, but by now you will have grasped my thesis, whether you agree with it or not. Either schools have caused these pathologies, or television has, or both. It's a simple matter of arithmetic—between schooling and television, all the time the children have is eaten up. There simply isn't enough other time in the experience of our kids for there to be other significant causes.

6.

What can be done?

First, we need a ferocious national debate that doesn't quit, day after day, year after year, the kind of continuous debate that journalism finds boring. We need to scream and argue about this school thing until it is fixed or broken beyond repair, one or the other. If we can fix it, fine; if we cannot, then the success of home-schooling shows a different road that has great promise. Pouring the money we now pour into schooling back into family education might cure two ailments with one medicine, repairing families as it repairs children.

Genuine reform is possible but it shouldn't cost anything. More money and more people pumped into this sick institution will only make it sicker. We need to rethink the fundamental premises of schooling and decide *what* it is we want all children to learn and *why*. For 140 years this nation has tried to impose objectives downward from a lofty command center made up of "experts," a central elite of social engineers. It hasn't worked. It won't work. And it is a gross betrayal of the democratic promise that once made this nation a noble experiment. The Russian attempt to create Plato's republic in Eastern Europe has exploded before our eyes; our own attempt to impose the same sort of central orthodoxy using the schools as an instrument is also coming apart at the seams, albeit more slowly and painfully. It doesn't work because its fundamental premises are mechanical, anti-human, and hostile to family life. Lives can be controlled by machine education but they will always fight back with weapons of social pathology: drugs, violence, self-destruction, indifference, and the symptoms I see in the children I teach.

7.

It's high time we looked backwards to regain an educational philosophy that works. One I like particularly well has been a favorite of the ruling classes of Europe for thousands of years. I use as much of it as I can manage in my own teaching, as much, that is, as I can get away with, given the present institution of compulsory schooling. I think it works just as well for poor children as for rich ones.

At the core of this elite system of education is the belief that self-knowledge is the only basis of true knowledge. Everywhere in this sytem, at every age, you will find arrangements that work to place the child *alone* in an unguided setting with a problem to solve. Sometimes the problem is fraught with great risks, such as the problem of galloping a horse or making it jump, but that, of course, is a problem successfully solved by thousands of elite children before the age of ten. Can you imagine anyone who had mastered such a challenge ever lacking confidence in his ability to do anything? Sometimes the problem is the problem of mastering solitude, as Thoreau did at Walden Pond, or Einstein did in the Swiss customs house.

Right now we are taking from our children all the time that they need to develop self-knowledge. That has to stop. We have to invent school experiences that give a lot of that time back. We need to trust children from a very early age with independent study, perhaps arranged in school, but which takes place *away* from the institutional setting. We need to invent curricula where each kid has a chance to develop private uniqueness and self-reliance.

A short time ago I took $70 and sent a twelve-year-old girl from my class, with her non-English-speaking mother, on a bus down the New Jersey coast to take the police chief of Seabright to lunch and apologize for polluting his beach with a discarded Gatorade bottle. In exchange for this public apology I had arranged with the police chief for the girl to have a one-day apprenticeship in small town police procedures. A few days later two more of my twelve-year-old kids travelled alone from Harlem to West Thirty-first street where they began an apprenticeship with a newspaper editor; later three of my kids found themselves in the middle of the Jersey swamps at six in the morning, studying the mind of a trucking company president as he dispatched eighteen-wheelers to Dallas, Chicago, and Los Angeles.

Are these "special" children in a "special" program? Well, in one sense yes, but nobody knows about this program but myself and the kids. They're just nice kids from central Harlem, bright and alert, but so badly schooled when they came to me that most of them couldn't add or subtract with any fluency. And not a single one knew the population of New York City or how far New York is from California.

Does that worry me? Of course; but I am confident that as they gain self-knowledge they'll also become self-teachers—and only self-teaching has any lasting value.

We've got to give kids independent time right away because that is the key to self-knowledge, and we must reinvolve them with the real world as fast as possible so that the independent time can be spent on something other than abstraction. This is an emergency; it requires drastic action to correct.

8.

What else does a restructured school system need? It needs to stop being a parasite on the working community. Of all the pages in the human ledger, only our tortured country has warehoused children and asked nothing of them in service of the general good. For a while I think we need to make community service a required part of schooling. Besides the experience in acting unselfishly that it will teach, it is the quickest way to give young children real responsibility in the mainstream of life.

For five years I ran a guerrilla school program where I had every kid, rich and poor, smart and dipsy, give 320 hours a year of hard community service. Dozens of those kids came back to me years later, grown up, and told me that the experience of helping someone else had changed their lives. It had taught them to see in new ways, to rethink goals and values. It happened when they were thirteen, in my Lab School program, and was only possible because my rich school district was in chaos. When "stability" returned, the Lab closed. It was too successful with a widely mixed group of kids, at too small a cost, to be allowed to continue.

Independent study, community service, adventures and experience, large doses of privacy and solitude, a thousand different apprenticeships, the one-day variety or longer—these are all powerful, cheap, and effective ways to start a real reform of schooling. But no large-scale reform is ever going to work to repair our damaged children and our damaged society until we force open the idea of "school" to include *family* as the main engine of education. If we use schooling to break children away from parents—and make no mistake, that has been the central function of schools since John Cotton announced it as the purpose of the Bay Colony schools in 1650 and Horace Mann announced it as the purpose of Massachusetts schools in 1850 - we're going to continue to have the horror show we have right now.

The "Curriculum of Family" is at the heart of any good life. We've gotten away from that curriculum; it's time to return to it. The way to sanity in education is for our schools to take the lead in releasing the stranglehold of institutions on family life, to promote during schooltime confluences of parent and child that will strengthen family bonds. That was my real purpose in sending the girl and her mother down the Jersey coast to meet the police chief.

I have many ideas for formulating a family curriculum and my guess is that a lot of you have many ideas, too. Our greatest problem in getting the kind of grassroots thinking going that could reform schooling is that we have large, vested interests preempting all the air time and profiting from schooling as it is, despite rhetoric to the contrary.

We have to demand that new voices and new ideas get a hearing, my ideas and yours. We've all had a bellyful of authorized voices mediated by television and the press; a decade-long free-for-all debate is what is called for now, not any more "expert" opinions. Experts in education have never been right; their "solutions" are expensive, self-serving, and always involve further centralization. We've seen the results.

It's time for a return to democracy, individuality, and family.

THE GREEN MONONGAHELA

In the beginning I became a teacher without realizing it. At the time, I was growing up on the banks of the green Monongahela River forty miles southwest of Pittsburgh, and on the banks of that deep green and always mysterious river I became a student too, master of the flight patterns of blue dragonflies and cunning adversary of the iridescent ticks that infested the riverbank willows.

"Mind you watch the ticks, Jackie!" Grandmother Mossie would call as I headed for the riverbank, summer and winter, only a two-minute walk from Second Street, where I lived across the trolley tracks of Main Street and the Pennsylvania Railroad tracks that paralleled them. I watched the red and yellow ticks chewing holes in the pale green leaves as I ran to the riverbank. On the river I drank my first Iron City at eight, smoked every cigarette obtainable, and watched dangerous men and women make love there at night on blankets—all before I was twelve. It was my laboratory: I

Awarded First Prize, Geraldine Dodge Foundation–Columbia University National Essay Contest.

learned to watch closely and draw conclusions there.

How did the river make me a teacher? Listen. It was alive with paddle-wheel steamers in center channel, the turning paddles churning up clouds of white spray, making the green river boil bright orange where its chemical undercurrent was troubled; from shore you could clearly hear the loud *thump thump thump* on the water. From all over town young boys ran gazing in awe. A dozen times a day. No one ever became indifferent to them because nothing important can ever really be boring. You can see the difference, can't you? Between those serious boats and the truly boring spacecraft of the past few decades, just flying junk without a purpose a boy can believe in; it's hard to feign an interest even now that I teach for a living and would like to pretend for the sake of the New York kids who won't have paddle-wheelers in their lives. The rockets are dull toys children in Manhattan put aside the day after Christmas, never to touch again; the riverboats were serious magic, clearly demarcating the world of boys from the world of men. Lévi-Strauss would know how to explain.

In Monongahela by that river everyone was my teacher. Daily, it seemed to a boy, one of the mile-long trains would stop in town to take on water and coal or for some mysterious reason; the brakeman and engineer would step among snot-nosed kids and spin railroad yarns, let us run in and out of boxcars, over and under flatcars, tank cars, coal cars, and numbers of other specialty cars whose function we memorized as easily as we memorized enemy plane silhouettes. Once a year, maybe, we got taken into the caboose that reeked of stale beer to be offered a bologna on white bread sandwich. The anonymous men lectured, advised, and inspired the boys of Monongahela—it was as much their job as driving the trains.

Sometimes a riverboat would stop in mid-channel and discharge a crew, who would row to shore, tying their skiff to one of the willows. That was the excuse for every rickety skiff in the twelve-block-long town to fill up with kids, pulling like Vikings, sometimes with sticks instead of oars, to raid the "Belle of Pittsburgh" or "The Original River Queen." Some kind of natural etiquette was at work in Monongahela. The rules didn't need to be written down; if men had time they showed boys how to grow up. We didn't whine when our time was up—men had work to do—we understood that and scampered away, grateful for the flash of our own futures they had had time to reveal, however small it was.

I was arrested three times growing up in Monongahela, or rather, picked up by the police and taken to jail to await a visit from Pappy to spring me. I wouldn't trade those times for anything. The first time I was nine, caught on my belly under a parked car at night, half an hour after curfew; in 1943 blinds were always drawn in the Monongahela Valley for fear Hitler's planes would somehow find a way to reach across the Atlantic to our steel mills lining both banks of the river. The Nazis were apparently waiting for a worried mother to go searching for her child with a flashlight after curfew, then *whammo!* down would descend the Teutonic air fleet!

Charlie was the cop's name. Down to the lockup we went—no call to mother until Charlie diagrammed the deadly menace of Goering's Luftwaffe. What a geopolitics lesson that was! Another time I speared a goldfish in the town fishpond and was brought from jail to the library, where I was sentenced to read for a month about the lives of animals. Finally, on VJ Day—when the Japanese cried "Uncle!"—I accepted a dare and broke the window of the police cruiser with a slingshot. Confessing, I suffered my first encounter with employment to pay for the glass, becoming sweep-up boy in my grandfather's printing office at fifty cents a week.

After I went away to Cornell I saw Monongahela and its green river only one more time, when I went there after my freshman year to give blood to my dying grandfather, who lay in the town hospital, as strong in his dying as he had ever been in his living. In another room my grandmother lay dying. Both passed within twenty-four hours, my grandad, Harry Taylor Zimmer, Sr., taking my blood to his grave in the cemetery there. My family moved again and again and again, but in my own heart I never left Monongahela, where I learned to teach from being taught by everyone in town, where

I learned to teach work from being asked to shoulder my share of responsibility, even as a boy, and where I learned to find adventures I made myself from the everyday stuff around me—the river and the people who lived alongside it.

In 1964 I was making a lot of money. That's what I walked away from to become a teacher. I was a copywriter on the fast track in advertising, a young fellow with a knack for writing thirty-second television commercials. My work required about one full day a month to complete, the rest of the time being spent in power breakfasts, after-work martinis at Michael's Pub, keeping up with the shifting fortunes of about twenty agencies in order to gauge the right time to jump ship for more money, and endless parties that always seemed to culminate in colossal headaches.

It bothered me that all the urgencies of the job were generated externally, but it bothered me more that the work I was doing seemed to have very little importance—even to the people who were paying for it. Worst of all, the problems this work posed were cut from such a narrow spectrum that it was clear that past, present, and future were to be of a piece: a twenty-nine-year-old man's work was no different from a thirty-nine-year-old man's work, or a forty-nine-year-old man's work (though there didn't seem to be any forty-nine-year-old copywriters—I had no idea why not).

"I'm leaving," I said one day to the copy chief.

"Are you nuts, Jack? You'll get profit sharing this year. We can match any offer you've got. Leaving for who?"

"For nobody, Dan. I mean I'm going to teach junior high school."

"When you see your mother next, tell her for me she raised a moron. Christ! Are you going to be sorry! In New York City we don't have schools; we have pens for lost souls. Teaching is a scam, a welfare project for losers who can't do anything else!"

Round and round I went with my advertising colleagues for a few days. Their scorn only firmed my resolve; the riverboats and trains of Monongahela were working inside me. I needed something to do that wasn't absurd more than I needed another party or a new abstract number in my bankbook.

And so I became a junior high school substitute teacher, working the beat from what's now Lincoln Center to Columbia, my alma mater, and from Harlem to the South Bronx. After three months the dismal working conditions, the ugly rooms, the torn books, the repeated instances of petty complaints from authorities, the bells, the buzzers, the drab teacher food in the cafeterias, the unpressed clothing, the inexplicable absence of conversation about children among the teachers (to this day, after twenty-six years in the business, I can honestly say I have *never once* heard an extended conversation about children or about teaching theory in any teachers' rooms I've been in) had just about done me in.

In fact, on the very first day I taught I was attacked by a boy waving a chair above his head. It happened in the infamous junior school Wadleigh, on 113th Street. I was given the eighth grade typing class—seventy-five students and typewriters—with this one injunction: "Under no circumstances are you to allow them to type. You lack the proper license. Is that understood?" A man named Mr. Bash said that to me.

It couldn't have taken more than sixty seconds from the time I closed the door and issued the order not to type for one hundred and fifty hands to snake under the typewriter covers and begin to type. But not all at once—that would have been too easy. First, three machines began to *clack clack* from the right rear. Quick, who were the culprits? I would race to the corner screaming *stop!*—when suddenly, from behind my back, three other machines would begin! Whirling as only a young man can do, I caught one small boy in the act. Then, to a veritable symphony of machines clicking, bells ringing, platens being thrown, I hoisted the boy from his chair and announced at the top of my foolish lungs I would make an example of this miscreant.

"Look out!" a girl shouted, and I turned toward her voice just in time to see a large brother of the little fellow I held heading toward me with a chair raised above his head. Releasing his brother, I seized a chair myself and raised it aloft. A standoff! We regarded each other at a distance of about ten feet for what seemed forever, the class jeering and howling, when the room door opened and Assistant Principal Bash, the very man who'd given the no-typing order, appeared.

"Mr. Gatto, have these children been typing?"

"No, sir," I said, lowering my chair, "but I think they want to. What do you suggest they do instead?"

He looked at me for signs of impudence or insubordination for a second, then, as if thinking better of rebuking this upstart, he said merely, "Fall back on your resources," and left the room.

Most of the kids laughed—they'd seen this drama enacted before.

The situation was defused, but silently I dubbed Wadleigh the "Death School." Stopping by the office on my way home, I told the secretary not to call me again if they needed a sub.

The very next morning my phone rang at 6:30. "Are you available for work today, Mr. Gatto?" said the voice briskly.

"Who is this?" I asked suspiciously. (Ten schools were using me for sub work in those days, and each identified itself at once.)

"The law clearly states, Mr. Gatto, that we do not have to tell you who we are until you tell us whether you are available for work."

"Never mind," I bellowed, "there's only one school who'd pull such crap! The answer is *no!* I am never available to work in your pigpen school!" And I slammed the receiver back onto its cradle.

But the truth was none of the sub assignments were boat rides; schools had an uncanny habit of exploiting substitutes and providing no support for their survival. It's likely I'd have returned to advertising if a little girl, desperate to free herself from an intolerable situation, hadn't drawn me into her personal school nightmare and shown me how I could find my own significance in teaching, just as those strong men in the riverboats and trains had found their own significance, a currency all of us need for our self-esteem.

It happened this way. Occasionally I'd get a call from an elementary school. This particular day it was a third grade assignment at a school on 107th Street, which in those days was nearly one hundred percent non-Hispanic in its teaching staff, and 99% Hispanic in its student body.

Like many desperate teachers, I killed most of the day listening to the kids read, one after another, and expending most of my energy trying to shut the audience up. This class had a very low ranking, and no one was able to put more than three or four words together without stumbling. All of a sudden, though, a little girl named Milagros sailed through a selection without a mistake. After class I called her over to my desk and asked why she was in this class of bad readers. She replied that "they" (the administration) wouldn't let her out because, as they explained to her mother, she was really a bad reader who had fantasies of being a better reader than she was. "But look, Mr. Gatto, my brother is in the sixth grade, and I can read every word in his English book better than he can!"

I was a little intrigued, but truthfully not much. Surely the authorities knew what they were doing. Still, the little girl seemed so frustrated I invited her to calm down and read to me from the sixth grade book. I explained that if she did well, I would take her case to the principal. I expected nothing.

Milagros, on the other hand, expected justice. Diving into "The Devil and Daniel Webster," she polished off the first two pages without a gulp. My God, I thought, this is a real reader. What is she doing here? Well, maybe it was a simple accident, easily corrected. I sent her home, promising to argue her case. Little did I suspect what a hornet's nest my request to have Milagros moved to a better class would stir up.

"You have some nerve, Mr. Gatto. I can't remember when a substitute ever told me how to run my school before. Have you taken specialized courses in reading?"

"No."

"Well then, suppose you leave these matters to the experts!"

"But the kid can *read!*"

"What do you suggest?"

"I suggest you test her, and if she isn't a dummy, get her out of the class she's in!"

"I don't like your tone. None of our children are dummies, Mr. Gatto. And you will find that girls like Milagros have many ways to fool amateurs like yourself. This is a matter of a

child having memorized one story. You can see
if I had to waste my time arguing with people
like you I'd have no time left to run a school."

But, strangely, I felt self-appointed as the
girl's champion, even though I'd probably
never see her again.

I insisted, and the principal finally agreed to
test Milagros herself the following Wednesday
after school. I made it a point to tell the little
girl the next day. By that time I'd come to think
that the principal was probably right—she'd
memorized one story—but I still warned her
she'd need to know the vocabulary from the
whole advanced reader and be able to read any
story the principal picked, without hesitation.
My responsibility was over, I told myself.

The following Wednesday after school I
waited in the room for Milagros' ordeal to be
over. At 3:30 she shyly opened the door of the
room.

"How'd it go?" I asked.

"I don't know," she answered, "but I didn't
make any mistakes. Mrs. Hefferman was very
angry, I could tell."

I saw Mrs. Hefferman, the principal, early
the next morning before school opened. "It
seems we've made a mistake with Milagros,"
she said curtly. "She will be moved, Mr. Gatto.
Her mother has been informed."

Several weeks later, when I got back to the
school to sub, Milagros dropped by, telling me
she was in the fast class now and doing very
well. She also gave me a sealed card. When I
got home that night, I found it, unopened, in

my suitcoat pocket. I opened it and saw a gaudy birthday card with blue flowers on it. Opening the card, I read, "A teacher like you cannot be found. Signed. Your student, Milagros."

That simple sentence made me a teacher for life. It was the first praise I'd ever heard in my working existence that had any meaning. I never forgot it, though I never saw Milagros again and only heard of her again in 1988, twenty-four years later. Then one day I picked up a newspaper and read:

Occupational Teacher Award

Milagros Maldonado, United Federation of Teachers, has won the Distinguished Occupational Teacher Award of the State Education Department for "demonstrated achievement and exemplary professionalism." A secretarial studies teacher at Norman Thomas High School, New York City, from which she graduated, Miss Maldonado was selected as a Manhattan Teacher of the Year in 1985 and was nominated the following year for the Woman of Conscience Award given by the National Council of Women.

Ah, Milagros, is it just possible that I was your Monongahela River? No matter, a teacher like you cannot be found.

WE NEED LESS SCHOOL,
NOT MORE

"We were making the future, " he said, and
hardly any of us troubled to think what
future we were making. And here it is!

—*The Sleeper Awakes*, H. G. Wells

A surprising number of otherwise sensible
people find it hard to see why the scope and
reach of our formal schooling networks should
not be increased—by extending the school day
or year, for instance—in order to provide an
economical solution to the problems posed by
the decay of the American family. One reason
for their preference, I think, is that they have
trouble understanding the real difference between
communities and networks, or even the difference
between families and networks.

Because of this confusion they conclude
that replacing a bad network with a good one
is the right way to go. Since I disagree so
strongly with the fundamental premise that
networks are workable substitutes for families,
and because from anybody's point of view a lot
more school is going to cost a lot more money,

I thought I'd tell you why, from a schoolteacher's perspective, we shouldn't be thinking of more school but of less.

People who admire our school institution usually admire networking in general and have an easy time seeing its positive side, but they overlook its negative aspect—that networks, even good ones, drain the vitality from communities and families. They provide *mechanical* ("by the numbers") solutions to human problems, when a slow, organic process of self-awareness, self- discovery, and cooperation is what is required if any solution is to stick.

Think of the challenge of losing weight. It's possible to employ mechanical tricks to do this quickly, but I'm told that ninety-five percent of the poor souls who do are only fooling themselves. The weight lost this way doesn't stay off, it comes back in a short time. Other network solutions are just as temporary: a group of law students may network to pass their college exams, but preparing a brief in private practice is often a solitary, lonely experience.

Aristotle saw, a long time ago, that fully participating in a complex range of human affairs was the only way to be become fully human; in *that* he differed from Plato. What is gained from consulting a specialist and surrendering all judgment is often more than outweighed by a permanent loss of one's own volition. This discovery accounts for the curious texture of *real* communication, where people argue with their doctors, lawyers, and ministers, tell craftsmen what they *want* instead of accepting what they get, frequently make their own food from scratch instead of buying it in a restaurant or defrosting it, and perform many similar acts of *participation.* A real community is, of course, a collection of real families who themselves function in this participatory way.

Networks, however, don't require the whole person, but only a narrow piece. If you function in a network it asks you to suppress all the parts of yourself except the network-interest part—a highly unnatural act although one you can get used to. In exchange, the network will deliver efficiency in the pursuit of some limited aim. This is in fact a devil's bargain, since on the promise of some future gain one must surrender the wholeness of one's present humanity. If you enter into too many of these bargains you will split youself into many specialized pieces, none of them completely human. And no time is available to reintegrate them. This, ironically, is the destiny of many successful networkers and doubtless generates much business for divorce courts and therapists of a variety of persuasions.

The fragmentation caused by excessive networking creates diminished humanity, a sense our lives are out of control because they are. If we face the present school and community crisis squarely, with hopes of finding a better way, we need to accept that schools, as networks, create a large part of the agony of modern life. We don't need more schooling, we need less.

I expect you'll want some proof of that, even though the million or so people participating in education at home these days have begun to nibble at the edge of everybody's consciousness and promise to bite their way into national attention when details of their success get around a little more. So for those of you who haven't heard that you don't need officially certified teachers in officially certified schools to get a good education, let me try to expose some of the machinery that makes certified schooling so bad. And remember, if you're thinking, "but it's *always* been that way,"...*that it really hasn't.*

Compulsory schooling in factory schools is a very recent, very Massachusetts/New York development. Remember, too, that until thirty-odd years ago you could escape mass-schooling *after* school; now it is much harder to escape because another form of mass-schooling, television, has spread all over the place to blot up any attention spared by school. So what was merely grotesque in our national treatment of the young before 1960 has become tragic now that mass commercial entertainment, as addictive as any other hallucinogenic drug, has blocked the escape routes from mass schooling.

It is a fact generally ignored when considering the communal nature of institutional families like schools, large corporations, colleges, armies, hospitals, and government agencies that they are not real communities at all, but networks. Unlike communities, networks—as I reminded you—have a very narrow way of allowing people to associate, and that way is always across a short spectrum of one, or at most a few, specific uniformities.

In spite of ritual moments like the Christmas party or the office softball game—when individual human components in the network "go home," they go home alone. And in spite of humanitarian support from fellow workers that eases emergencies—when people in networks suffer, they suffer alone, unless they have a family or community to suffer with them.

Even with college dorm "communities," those most engaging and intimate simulations of community imaginable, who among us has not experienced an awful realization after graduation that we cannot remember our friends' names or faces very well? Or who, if one can remember, feels much desire to renew those associations?

It is a puzzling development, as yet poorly understood, that the "caring" in networks is in some important way feigned. Not maliciously, but in spite of any genuine emotional attractions that might be there, human behavior in network situations often resembles a dramatic act—matching a script produced to meet the demands of a story. And, as such, the intimate moments in networks lack the sustaining value of their counterparts in community. Those of you who remember the wonderful closeness possible in army camp life or sports teams, and who have now forgotten those you were once close with, will understand what I mean. In contrast, have you ever forgotten an uncle or an aunt?

If the loss of true community entailed by masquerading in networks is not noticed in time, a condition arises in the victim's spirit very much like the "trout starvation" that used to strike wilderness explorers whose diet was made up exclusively of stream fish. While trout quell the pangs of hunger—and even taste good—the eater gradually suffers for want of sufficient nutrients.

Networks like schools are not communities, just as school training is not education. By preempting fifty percent of the total time of the young, by locking young people up with other young people exactly their own age, by ringing bells to start and stop work, by asking people to think about the same thing at the same time in the same way, by grading people the way we grade vegetables—and in a dozen other vile and stupid ways—network schools steal the vitality of communities and replace it with an ugly mechanism. No one survives these places with their humanity intact, not kids, not teachers, not administrators, and not parents.

A community is a place in which people face each other over time in *all* their human variety, good parts, bad parts, and all the rest. Such places promote the highest quality of life possible, lives of engagement and participation. This happens in unexpected ways, but it never happens when you've spent more than a decade listening to other people *talk* and trying to do what they tell you to do, trying to *please* them after the fashion of schools. It makes a real lifelong difference whether you avoid that training or it traps you.

An example might clarify this. Networks of urban reformers will convene to consider the problems of homeless vagrants, but a community will think of its vagrants as real people, not abstractions. Ron, Dave or Marty—a community will call its bums by their names. It makes a difference.

People interact on thousands of invisible pathways in a community, and the emotional payoff is correspondingly rich and complex. But networks can only manage a cartoon simulation of community and provide a very limited payoff.

I belong to some networks myself, of course, but the only ones I consider completely safe are the ones that reject their communal facade, acknowledge their limits, and concentrate solely on helping me do a specific and necessary task. But a vampire network like a school, which tears off huge chunks of time and energy needed for building community and family—and always asks for *more*—needs to have a stake driven through its heart and be nailed into its coffin. The feeding frenzy of formal schooling has already wounded us seriously in our ability to form families and communities, by bleeding away time we need with our children and our children need with us. That's why I say we need less school, not more.

Who can deny that networks can get some jobs done? They do. But they lack any ability to nourish their members emotionally. The extreme *rationality* at the core of networking is based on the same misperception of human nature the French Enlightenment and Comte were guilty of. At our best we human beings are much, much grander than merely rational; at our best we transcend rationality while incorporating its procedures into our lower levels of functioning. This is why computers will never replace people, for they are condemned to be rational, hence very limited.

Networks divide people, first from themselves and then from each other, on the grounds that this is the efficient way to perform a task. It may well be, but it is a lousy way to feel good about being alive. Networks make people lonely. They cannot correct their inhuman mechanism and still succeed as networks. Behind the anomaly that networks look like communities (but are not) lurks the grotesque secret of mass-schooling and the reason why enlarging the school domain will only aggravate the dangerous conditions of social disintegration it is intended to correct.

I want to repeat this until you are sick of hearing it. Networks do great harm by appearing enough like real communities to create expectations that they can manage human social and psychological needs. The reality is they cannot. Even associations as inherently harmless as bridge clubs, chess clubs, amateur acting groups, or groups of social activists will, if they maintain a pretense of whole friendship, ultimately produce that odd sensation familiar to all city dwellers of being lonely in the middle of a crowd. Which of us who frequently networks has not felt this sensation? Belonging to many networks does *not* add up to having a community, no matter how many you belong to or how often your telephone rings.

With a network, what you get at the beginning is all you ever get. Networks don't get better or worse; their limited purpose keeps them pretty much the same all the time, as there just isn't much development possible. The pathological sate which eventually develops out of these constant repetitions of thin human contact is a feeling that your "friends" and "colleagues" don't really care about you beyond what you can do for them, that they have no curiosity about the way you manage your life, no curiosity about your hopes, fears, victories, defeats. The real truth is that the "friends" falsely mourned for their indifference were never friends, only fellow networkers from whom in fairness little should be expected beyond attention to the common interest.

But given our unquenchable need for community and the unlikelihood of obtaining that community in a network, we are in such desperation of any solution that we are driven to deceive ourselves about the nature of these liasons. Whatever "caring" really means, it means something more than simple companionship or even the comradeship of shared interests.

2.

In the growth of human society, families came first, communities second, and only much later came the institutions set up by the community to serve it. Most institutional rhetoric—the proclaiming of what is important—borrows its values from those of individual families that work well together.

Particularly over the past century and a half in the United States, spokesmen for institutional life have demanded a role above and beyond service to families and communities. They have sought to command and prescribe as kings used to do, though there is an important difference. In the case of ancient kings, once beyond the range of their voices and trumpets you could usually do what you pleased; but in the case of modern institutions, the reach of technology is everywhere—there is no escape if the place where you live and the family you live in cannot provide sanctuary.

Institutions, say their political philosophers, are better at creating marching orders for the human race than families are, therefore they should no longer be expected to follow but should lead. Institutional leaders have come to regard themselves as great *synthetic fathers* to millions of *synthetic children*, by which I mean to all of us. This theory sees us bound together in some abstract family relationship in which the state is the true *mother* and *father*; hence it insists on our first and best loyalty.

"Ask not," said President Kennedy, "what
your country can do for *you*, but rather ask
what *you* can do for your country." Since the
"you" in question is both real and human, and
the country you are alleged to possess one of
the most extreme of verbal abstractions, it will
readily be seen that the president's injunction
is an expression of a synthetic family philosophy
which regards "nation" as possessing a claim
superior to the claim of "family". If you see
nothing wrong with this, then it is probable
you also believe that, with a little tinkering, our
schools will work just fine. But if you have a
queer feeling about the image of yourself and
family as appendages of an abstraction, then
we are on the same wavelength. In the latter
case, we are ready to consider that we may
need less school, not more.

3.

I want to examine the destructive effects the
false claim of institutional prerogative has on
both individual and family life, a destructiveness
equally profound whether the claim comes
from a government, a corporation, or from
some other form of network.

If we return to our original discussion of
networks, it will be clear that every one of our
national institutions is a place where men,
women, and children are isolated according to
some limited aspect of their total humanity: by
age, and a few other considerations, in the case
of compulsory schooling, and by various other

sorting mechanisms in the other institutional arenas.

If performance within these narrow confines is conceived to be the supreme measure of success, if, for instance, an *A* average is accounted the central purpose of adolescent life—the requirements for which take most of the time and attention of the aspirant—and the worth of the individual is reckoned by victory or defeat in this abstract pursuit, then a social machine has been constructed which, by attaching purpose and meaning to essentially meaningless and fantastic behavior, will certainly dehumanize students, alienate them from their own human nature, and break the natural connection between them and their parents, to whom they would otherwise look for significant affirmations.

Welcome to the world of mass-schooling, which sets this goal as its supreme achievement. Are you sure we want more of it?

As we approach the twenty-first century it is correct to say that the United States has become a nation of institutions, whereas it used to be a nation of communities. Large cities have great difficulty supporting healthy community life, partly because of the coming and going of strangers, partly because of space constrictions, partly because of poisoned environments, but mostly because of the constant competition of institutions and networks for the custody of children and old people, for monopolizing the time of everyone else in between. By isolating young and old from the

working life of places, and by isolating the
working population from the lives of young and
old, a fundamental disconnection of the generations has occurred. The griefs that arise from
this have no synthetic remedy, and no vibrant,
satisfying communities can come into being
where young and old are locked away.

Here and there mutilated versions of community struggle to survive, as in places where
cultural homogeneity has been fiercely pro-
tected—such as in Bensonhurst in Brooklyn or
Polish Hill in Pittsburgh—but in the main,
"community" in cities and suburbs is a thin
illusion, confined to simulated events like
street festivals. If you have moved from one
neighborhood to another or from one suburb
to another and have quickly forgotten the
friends you left behind, then you will have
experienced the phenomenon I refer to. Over
ninety percent of the United States' population
now lives inside fifty urban aggregations.
Having been concentrated there as the end
product of fairly well understood historical
processes, they are denied a reciprocal part in
any continuous, well-articulated community.
They are profoundly alienated from their own
human interests. What else could it mean that
only half our eligible citizens are registered to
vote? And that of those a barely fifty percent *do*
vote? In two-party jurisdictions a trifle over
one-eighth of the citizenry is thus sufficient to
elect public officials, assuming the vote splits
fairly evenly. We've come a long way down the
road to redefining as an option what used to be

regarded as a duty, but that is what alienation from community life quickly accomplishes: indifference to almost everything.

When one is offered institutional simulations of community, a steady diet of networks—involuntary like schools, or "voluntary" like isolated workplaces divorced from human variety—basic human needs are placed in the gravest jeopardy, a danger magnified many times in the case of children. Institutional goals, however sane and well-intentioned, are unable to harmonize deeply with the uniqueness of individual human goals. No matter how good the individuals are who manage an institution, institutions lack a conscience because they measure by accounting methods. Institutions are not the sum total of their personnel, or even of their leadership, but are independent of both and will exist after management has been completely replaced. They are ideas come to life, ideas in whose service all employees are but servomechanisms. The deepest purposes of these gigantic networks is to regulate and to make uniform. Since the logic of family and community is to give scope to variety around a central theme, whenever institutions intervene significantly in personal affairs they cause much damage. By redirecting the focus of our lives from families and communities to institutions and networks, we, in effect, anoint a machine our king.

4.

Nearly a century ago a French sociologist wrote that every institution's unstated first goal is to survive and grow, *not* to undertake the mission it has nominally staked out for itself. Thus the first goal of a government postal service is not to deliver the mail; it is to provide protection for its employees and perhaps a modest status ladder for the more ambitious ones. The first goal of a permanent military organization is not to defend national security, but to secure, in perpetuity, a fraction of the national wealth to distribute to its personnel.

It was this philistine potential, teaching the young *for pay*, would inevitably expand into an institution for the protection of teachers, not students, that made Socrates condemn the Sophists so strongly long ago in ancient Greece.

If this view of things troubles you, think of the New York City public school system, where I work, one of the largest business organizations on planet Earth. While the education administered by this abstract parent is ill-regarded by everybody, the institution's right to *compel* its clientele to accept such dubious service is still guaranteed by the police. And forces are gathering to expand its reach still further—in the face of every evidence that it has been a disaster throughout its history.

What gives the atmosphere of remote country towns and other national backwaters a peculiarly heady quality of fundamental difference is not simply a radical change of scenery from city or suburb, but the promise offered of near-freedom from institutional intervention in family life. Big Father doesn't watch over such places closely. Where his presence is felt most is still in the schools, which even there grind out their relentless message of anger, envy, competition, and caste-verification in the form of grades and "classes." But a homelife and community exist there as antidote to the poison.

This business we call "education," when we mean "schooling," makes an interesting example of network values in conflict with traditional community values. For one hundred and fifty years institutional education has seen fit to offer as its main purpose the preparation for economic success. Good education = good job, good money, good *things*. This has become the universal national banner, hoisted by Harvards as well as high schools. This prescription makes both parent and student easier to regulate and intimidate as long as the connection goes unchallenged either for its veracity or in its philosophical truth. Interestingly enough, the American Federation of Teachers identifies one of its missions as persuading the business community to hire and promote on the basis of school grades so that the grades = money formula will obtain, just as it was made to obtain for medicine and law after years of political lobbying. So far, the common sense of businesspeople has kept them hiring and promoting the old-fashioned way, using peformance and private judgment as the preferred measures, but they may not resist much longer.

The absurdity of defining education as an economic good becomes clear if we ask ourselves what is gained by perceiving education as a way to enhance even further the runaway consumption that threatens the earth, the air, and the water of our planet? Should we continue to teach people that they can buy happiness in the face of a tidal wave of evidence that they cannot? Shall we ignore the evidence that drug addiction, alcoholism, teenage suicide, divorce, and other despairs are pathologies of the prosperous much more than they are of the poor?

On this question of meanings we've hidden from ourselves for so long hangs both an understanding of the illness that is killing us and the cure we are searching for. What, after all this time, is the purpose of mass-schooling supposed to be? Reading, writing, and arithmetic can't be the answer, because properly approached those things take less than a hundred hours to transmit—and we have abundant evidence that each is readily self-taught in the right setting and time.

Why, then, are we locking these kids up in an involuntary network with strangers for twelve years? Surely not so a few of them can get rich? Even if it worked that way, and I doubt that it does, why wouldn't any sane community look on such an education as positively wrong? It divides and classifies

people, demanding that they compulsively
compete with each other and publicly labels
the losers by literally de-grading them, identifying
them as "low-class" material. The bottom line
for the winners is that they can buy more *stuff*!
I don't believe that anyone who thinks about it
feels comfortable with such a silly conclusion.
I can't help feeling that if we could only answer
the question of what it is that we want from
these kids we lock up, we would suddenly see
where we took a wrong turn. I have enough
faith in American imagination and resourcefulness to believe that at that point we'd come up
with a better way—in fact, a whole supermarket
of better ways.

One thing I do know: most of us who've had
a taste of loving families, even a little taste,
want our kids to be part of one. One other thing
I know is that eventually you have to come to
be part of a *place*— part of its hills and streets
and waters and people—or you will live a very,
very sorry life as an exile forever. *Discovering
meaning for yourself*, and discovering satisfying
purpose for yourself, is a big part of what
education is. How this can be done by locking
children away from the world is beyond me.

5.

An important difference between communities
and institutions is that communities have
natural limits; they *stop* growing or they die.
There's a good reason for this: in the best
communities everyone is a special person who

sooner or later impinges on everyone else's consciousness. The effects of this constant attention make all, rich or poor, feel important, because the only way importance is perceived is by having other folks pay attention to you. You can *buy* attention, of course, but it's not the same thing. Pseudo community life, where you live around others without noticing them, and where you are constantly being menaced in some way by strangers you find offensive, is exactly the opposite. In pseudo community life you *are* anonymous for the most part, and you want to be because of various dangers other people may present if they notice your existence. Almost the only way you can get attention in a pseudo community is to buy it, because the prevailing atmosphere is one of indifference. A pseudo community is just a different kind of network—its friendships and loyalties are transient; its problems are universally considered to be someone else's problems (someone else who should be *paid* to solve them); its young and old are largely regarded as annoyances; and the most commonly shared dream is to get out to a better place, to "trade up" endlessly.

Unlike true communities, pseudo communities and other comprehensive networks like schools expand indefinitely, just as long as they can get away with it. "More" may not be "better," but more is always more profitable for the people who make a living out of networking. That is what is happening today behind the cry to expand schooling even further: a great many people are going to make a great deal of money if growth can be continued.

Unlike the intricate, sometimes unfathomable satisfactions of community and family life, the successes of networks are always measured in mathematical displays of one-upmanship: How many *A's*? How much weight lost? How many inquiries generated? Competition is the network's lifeblood, and the precision suggested by the numerical ranking of performance is its preferred style.

The quality-competition of businesses, when it actually happens, is generally a good thing for customers; it keeps businesses on their toes, doing their best. The competition inside an institution like a school isn't the same thing at all. What is competed for in a school is the favor of a teacher, and that can be won or lost by too many subjective parameters to count; it is always a little arbitrary and sometimes a lot more pernicious than that. It gives rise to envy, dissatisfaction, and a belief in magic. Teachers, too, must compete for the arbitrarily dispensed favor of administrators, which carries the promise of good or bad classes, good or bad rooms, access to or denial of tools, and other hostages to obedience, deference, and subordination. The culture of schools only coheres in response to a web of material rewards and punishments: *A's*, *F's*, bathroom passes, gold stars, "good" classes, access to a photocopy machine. Everything we know about *why* people drive themselves to know things and do their best is contradicted inside these places.

Truth itself is another important dividing line between communities and networks. If you don't keep your word in a community everyone finds out, and you have a major problem thereafter. But lying for personal advantage is the operational standard in all large institutions; it is considered part of the game in schools. Parents, for the most part, are lied to or told half-truths, as they are usually considered adversaries. At least that's been true in every school I ever worked in. Only the most foolish employees don't have recourse to lying; the penalties for being caught hardly exist—and the rewards for success can be considerable. Whistle-blowing against institutional malpractice is always a good way to get canned or relentlessly persecuted. Whistle-blowers never get promoted in any institution because, having served a public interest once, they may well do it again.

The Cathedral of Rheims is the best evidence I know of what a community can do and what we stand to lose when we don't know the difference between these human miracles and the social machinery we call networks. Rheims was built without power tools by people working day and night for a hundred years. Everybody worked willingly, nobody was slave labor. No school taught cathedral building as a subject.

What possessed people to work together for a hundred years? Whatever it was looks like something worth educating ourselves about. We know the workers were profoundly united as families and as friends, and as friends they knew what they really wanted in the way of a church. Popes and archbishops had nothing to do with it; Gothic architecture itself was invented out of sheer aspiration; the Gothic cathedral stands like a lighthouse illuminating what is possible in the way of uncoerced human union. It provides a benchmark against which our own lives can be measured.

At Rheims, the serfs and farmers and peasants filled gigantic spaces with the most incredible stained glass windows in the world, but they never bothered to sign even one of them. No one knows who designed them or made them, because our modern form of institutional boasting did not yet exist as a corruption of communitarian feeling. After all these centuries they still announce what being human really means.

6.

Communities are collections of families and friends who find major meaning in extending the family association to a band of honorary brothers and sisters. They are complex relationships of commonality and obligation which generalize to others beyond the perimeter of the homestead.

When the integration of life that comes from being part of a family in a community is unattainable, the only alternative, apart from accepting a life in isolation, is to search for an artificial integration into one of the many expressions of network currently available. It's a bad trade. Artificial integration that controls human association—think of those college dorms or fraternities—appears strong but is actually quite weak; seems close-knit but in reality its bonds are loose; suggests durability but is usually transient. And it is most often badly adjusted to what people need although it masquerades as being exactly what they need.

Welcome to the world of school. We should begin thinking about school reform by stopping these places from functioning like cysts, impenetrable, insular bodies that take our money, our children, and our time and give nothing back. Do we really want more of it?

In recent years I've given much thought to the problem of turning the compulsory school network into some kind of emotionally rewarding community, because a move seems to be afoot to do the reverse, to enlarge substantially the bite that schooling takes out of a young person's family time, community time, and private time. Trial balloons are floated about constantly in the press and on TV; that means that some important groups are preparing to extend the reach of compulsory schooling in the face of its genuinely ghastly record. My Jewish friends would call that *chutzpah*, but I take it as an index of just how confident these people are that they can pull it off.

Schools, I hear it argued, would make better sense and be better value as nine-to-five operations or even nine-to-nine ones, working year-round. We're not a farming community anymore, I hear, that we need to give kids time off to tend the crops. This new-world-order schooling would serve dinner, provide evening recreation, offer therapy, medical attention, and a whole range of other services, which would convert the institution into a true synthetic family for children, better than the original one for many poor kids, it is said; and this will level the playing field for the sons and daughters of weak families.

Yet it appears to me as a schoolteacher that schools are already a major cause of weak families and weak communities. They separate parents and children from vital interaction with each other and from true curiosity about each other's lives. Schools stifle family originality by appropriating the critical time needed for any sound idea of family to develop—then they blame the family for its failure to be a family. It's like a malicious person lifting a photograph from the developing chemicals too early, then pronouncing the photographer incompetent.

A Massachusetts Senator said a while ago that his state had a higher literacy rate before it adopted compulsory schooling than after. It's certainly an idea worth considering: schools reached their maximum efficiency long ago, and that "more" for schools will make things worse, instead of better.

7.

Whatever an education is, it should make you a unique individual, not a conformist; it should furnish you with an original spirit with which to tackle the big challenges; it should allow you to find values which will be your road map through life; it should make you spiritually rich, a person who loves whatever you are doing, wherever you are, whomever you are with; it should teach you what is important, how to live and how to die.

What's gotten in the way of education in the United States is a theory of social engineering that says there is *one right way* to proceed with growing up. That's an ancient Egyptian idea symbolized by the pyramid with an eye on top that's on the other side of George Washington on our one-dollar bill. Everyone is a stone defined by position on the pyramid. This theory has been presented in many different ways, but at bottom it signals the worldview of minds obsessed with the control of other minds, obsessed by dominance and strategies of intervention to maintain that dominance.

It might have worked for the Pharaohs but it certainly hasn't worked very well for us. Indeed, nothing in the historical record provides evidence that any one idea should dominate the developmental time of all the young, and yet aspirants to monopolize this time have never been closer to winning the prize. The humming of the great hive society foreseen by Francis Bacon and by H.G. Wells in *The*

Sleeper Awakes has never sounded louder than it does to us right now.

The heart of a defense for the cherished American ideals of privacy, variety, and individuality lies in the way we bring up our young. *Children learn what they live.* Put kids in a class and they will live out their lives in an invisible cage, isolated from their chance at community; interrupt kids with bells and horns all the time and they will learn that nothing is important; force them to plead for the natural right to the toilet and they will become liars and toadies; ridicule them and they will retreat from human association; shame them and they will find a hundred ways to get even. The habits taught in large-scale organizations are deadly.

On the other hand, individuality, family, and community are, *by definition*, expressions of singular organization, never of "one-right-way" thinking on the grand scale. Private time is absolutely essential if a private identity is going to develop, and private time is equally essential to the development of a code of private values, without which we aren't really individuals at all. Children and families need some relief from government surveillance and intimidation if original expressions belonging to *them* are to develop. Without these freedom has no meaning.

The lesson of my teaching life is that both the theory and structure of mass-education are fatally flawed; they cannot work to support the democratic logic of our national idea because they are unfaithful to the democratic principle. The democratic principle is still the best idea for a nation, even though we aren't living up to it right now.

Mass-education cannot work to produce a fair society because its daily practice is practice in rigged competition, suppression, and intimidation. The schools we've allowed to develop can't work to teach nonmaterial values, the values which give meaning to everyone's life, rich or poor, because the structure of schooling is held together by a Byzantine tapestry of reward and threat, of carrots and sticks. Working for official favor, grades, or other trinkets of subordination; these have no connection with education—they are the paraphernalia of servitude, not freedom.

Mass-schooling damages children. We don't need any more of it. And under the guise that it is the same thing as education, it has been picking our pockets just as Socrates predicted it would thousands of years ago. One of the surest ways to recognize education is that it doesn't cost very much; it doesn't depend on expensive toys or gadgets. The experiences that produce it and the self-awareness that propels it are nearly free. It is hard to turn a dollar on education. But schooling is a wonderful hustle, getting sharper all the time.

Sixty-five years ago Bertrand Russell, probably the greatest mathematician of this century, its greatest philosopher, and a close relation of the King of England to boot, saw that mass-schooling in the United States had a profoundly

anti-democratic intent, that it was a scheme to
artificially deliver national unity by eliminating
human variation and by eliminating the forge
that produces variation: the family. According
to Lord Russell, mass-schooling produced a
recognizably *American* student: anti-intellectual,
superstitious, lacking self-confidence, and with
less of what Russell called "inner freedom"
than his or her counterpart in any other nation
he knew of, past or present. These schooled
children became citizens, he said, with a
thin "mass character," holding excellence and
aesthetics equally in contempt, inadequate to
the personal crises of their lives.

American national unity has always been
the central problem of American life. It was
inherent in our synthetic beginnings and in
the conquest of a continental landmass. It was
true in 1790 and it is just as true, perhaps even
truer, two hundred years later. Somewhere
around the time of the Civil War we began to
try shortcuts to get the unity we wanted faster,
by artificial means. Compulsory schooling was
one of those shortcuts, perhaps the most
important one. "Take hold the children!" said
John Cotton back in colonial Boston, and that
seemed such a good idea that eventually the
people who looked at "unity" almost as if it
were a religious idea did just that. It took thirty
years to beat down a fierce opposition, but by
the 1880s it had come to pass—"they" had the
children. For the last one hundred and ten
years, the "one-right-way" crowd has been

trying to figure out what to do with the children and they still don't know.

Perhaps it is time to try something different. "Good fences make good neighbors," said Robert Frost. The natural solution to learning to live together in a community is *first* to learn to live apart as individuals and as families. Only when you feel good about yourself can you feel good about others.

But we attacked the problem of unity mechanically, as though we could force an engineering solution by crowding the various families and communities under the broad, homogenizing umbrella of institutions like compulsory schools. In working this scheme the democratic ideas that were the only justification for our national experiment were betrayed.

The attempt at a shortcut continues, and it ruins families and communities now, just as it always did then. Rebuild these things and young people will begin to educate themselves— with our help—just as they did at the nation's beginning. They don't have anything to work for now except money, and that's never been a first-class motivator. Break up these institutional schools, decertify teaching, let anyone who has a mind to teach bid for customers, privatize this whole business—trust the free market system. I know it's easier to say than to do, but what other choice do we have? We need less school, not more.

reform, where serious mistakes are self-limiting and quickly, in historical terms, foreclosed by natural market mechanisms. Come with me to the coasts of Colonial New England, to towns like Salem and Marblehead, Framingham and Dedham, Wellfleet and Provincetown. Consider a different perspective that grew out of the soil of a New World, a perspective that shocked other nations with the productivity of its genius.

This new system began with the first Puritan church at Salem, organized in 1629 by the so-called "Salem Procedure." No "higher-up" was around to approve the selection of the church authorities, so the congregation took that responsibility upon themselves. With that simple act, they took power that had traditionally belonged to some certified expert and placed it in the hands of people who went to church. That was the sole criterion of governance: that a voter took going to church seriously and joined a congregation as evidence. It was an act of monumental localism. For the next two hundred years that simple shedding of traditional authority corroded the monopoly power of the state and church to broadcast uniform versions of the truth. Each separate congregation took a vigorous role in particularizing its own parish through debate of lay members, not through the centralization inherent in pronouncement by outside authority. Each separate congregation took on responsibility for solving its own problems—whether of education, economics, or doctrine—rather than submitting to the old authority of England or to the new aristocracy of expertise.

Last fall I spoke in the town of Dedham at a church built in 1638, only nine years after the *Arbella* brought the Nonconformists to Boston. The church I spoke in was a Unitarian-Universalist parish, but it had originally been Congregational. White spire, strikingly plain, graceful lines—the simplicity and rightness of Congregational church architecture is absolutely unmistakable, remarkable, and uniform. You may or may not be aware that the style of worship that went with this style of architecture was the original and exclusive religion of the Massachusetts Bay Colony, from the Salem Procedure until 1834, over two hundred years of what seems on the surface to be a "one right way" religion. You were either a Congregationalist, or you weren't anything you dared speak of in public, at least without risk of being shunned, persecuted, or even burned at the stake. So far this sounds even worse than the school monopoly that ruins us, doesn't it?

These Congregationalists were so jealously protective of their monopoly that one hundred and seventy years ago, when Lyman Beecher got word that Unitarians were on their way out from the bowels of hell, he rode through the streets just like Paul Revere warning, "The Unitarians are coming! The Unitarians are coming!" You'll gather Parson Beecher wasn't exactly thrilled with their advent. But an amazing thing happened over the next century.

The Congregationalists slowly changed their minds *without being forced to do so.* By the end of the 1800s, the Unitarians were well respected throughout New England.

Most people think of Colonial New England as the greatest period of conformity this country has ever seen. But the *nature* of Congregationalism hides a very great irony. Structurally, this way of life *demands individuality, not regimentation.* The service is almost free of liturgy, emphasizing local preaching about local issues. This virtually guarantees *dissonance* inside the congregation. The constant struggle for light by every church member acting as his or her own priest, his or her own expert, invariably leads to progress toward truth. Why do I say that? Well, what I've just described is the process that Aristotle or Karl Marx or Thomas Hobbes or any of a large number of creative thinkers have called "the dialectic." The Congregational procedure was dialectical down to its roots, in a way acutely hostile to hierarchical thinking.

Central planners of any period despise the dialectic because it gets in the way of efficiently broadcasting "one right way" to do things. Half a century ago Bertrand Russell remarked that the United States was the only major country on earth that deliberately avoided teaching its children to think dialectically. He was talking about twentieth century America, of course, the land of compulsory government schooling, not the New England of Congregational distinction. Did you wonder where "Yankees" got their lasting reputation for stubbornness, orneriness, and shrewd hair-splitting? Now you know. Roger Williams saw as clearly as any person of his time and recognized the inevitable connection between dissonance and quality of life. You can't have one without the other.

Much recent scholarship has shown the towns of Massachusetts in the seventeenth century not to be uniform at all, but to be laboratories of local choice and style. Each had considerable flexibility to deviate from what might have been central governmental rule. The town of Dedham, where I spoke last fall, drew its original settlers from East Anglia in England, a place that favored private ownership and individual choice. The institutions of East Anglia quickly established themselves in the New World too. On the other hand, Sudbury, the town next to Dedham, had been populated by colonists of Saxon and Celtic background, who traditionally shared work in common. Just as they had done in Britain they held open fields in common in America. In Colonial Massachusetts, then, there was creative tension between the common culture of the region and the local village culture. Like tension in music or poetry between a regular pattern and creative departures from it, this tension among the small towns and among the different congregations and inside each separate congregation produced an astonishing energy, a fertile and idiosyncratic peculiarity that characterized the particular genius that characterized colonial Massachusetts.

Now I want us to examine something that seems embarrassing in New England civil life; and yet, paradoxically, I think it hides a secret of great power, which the social engineers who built and maintain our government monopoly schools are forced to overlook. *Each town was able to exclude people it didn't like!* People were able to *choose* whom they wanted to work with, to sort themselves into a living curriculum that worked for them. The words of the first Dedham charter catch this feeling perfectly; the original settlers wanted to shut out (and did) "people whose dispositions do not suit us, whose society will be hurtful to us." So in a funny way these early towns functioned like selective *clubs* or colleges, like MIT and Harvard do today, narrowing human differences down to a range that could be managed by them humanely. If you consider the tremendous stresses the dialectical process sets up anyway—where all people are their own priests, their own final masters—it's hard to see how a congregational society can do otherwise. If you have to accept everyone, no matter how hostile they may be to your own personality, philosophy, or mission, then an operation would quickly become paralyzed by fatal disagreements. The common causes and purposes that mark human association at its best must degrade into those few innocuous undertakings that have no political dimension, if such can be found.

It's a subtle distinction: living dialectically as the New Englanders did produces spectacular accomplishments and brings out strong qualities of character and mind in individuals, but it isn't possible to manage where the whole catalogue of human beings is thrown together haphazardly or forced together, as it is in government monopoly school life. To prevent chaos in these places, management must aim, by hook or by crook, to make everything—time, space, texts, and procedures—as uniform as possible. The Greeks had a story about a man who did that, named Procustes. He cut or stretched travellers to fit his guest bed. The system worked perfectly, but it played havoc with the traveller.

These New Englanders invented a system where people who wanted to live and work together could do so. Yet the whole region seemed to prosper in wonderful ways: materially, intellectually, and socially. It was almost as if by taking care of your own business you succeeded in some magical fashion in taking care of public business too. The habits of self-reliance, self-respect, fearlessness, democracy, and local loyalty produced good citizens. Government monopoly schools use a different blueprint these days, of course. People are drawn willy-nilly out of large "catchment" areas and dumped into compartments together according to similar scores on standardized tests. There they are exhorted to perform and behave according to the specifications of strangers. Christopher Lasch says in *The True and Only Heaven*:

> The capacity for loyalty is stretched too thin when it tries to attach itself to the hypothetical solidarity of the human race. It needs to attach itself to specific people and specific places, not to an abstract ideal of universal human rights. We love particular men and women, not humanity in general.

This catches a piece of what's wrong with compulsory schools as large as New England towns, schools that don't allow choice of curricula, philosophy, or companions. Wendell Berry catches another piece of it in a letter to a magazine editor:

> I don't think 'global thinking' is futile, I think it is impossible. You can't think about what you don't know and nobody knows this planet. Some people know a little about a few small parts of it....The people who think globally do so by abstractly and statistically reducing the globe to quantities. Political tyrants and industrial exploiters have done this most successfully. Their concepts and their greed are abstract and their abstractions lead with terrifying directness and simplicity to acts that are invariably destructive. If you want to do good and preserving acts you must think and act locally. The effort to do good acts gives the global game away. You can't do a good act that is global...a good act, to be good, must be acceptable to what Alexander Pope called "the genius of the place." This calls for local knowledge, local skills, and local love that virtually none of us

> has, and that none of us can get by thinking
> globally. We can get it only by a local fidelity
> that we would have to maintain through
> several lifetimes....I don't wish to be loved by
> people who don't know me; if I were a planet
> I would feel exactly the same way.

Local skills, local knowledge, local love, and local fidelity were what the forge of Congregationalism in New England produced best, but there was a negative side to this localism too.

The religious discrimination of early New England was a way of ensuring enough local harmony that a community of people who suited each other could arise bearing a common vision. Here is a scene from three hundred years ago in the town of Dedham, Massachusetts, which could have been witnessed from the very church where I spoke: three Quaker women are stripped to the waist and whipped the length of town, tied to the tail of a cart. It would be an understatement to say that such treatment underlined the fact that the Quaker disposition was not one of those suited to Dedham. But then, for that matter, neither was the Presbyterian disposition. John Milton himself had written that the "new Presbyter is but old Priest writ large," and so all Presbyterians were driven off to the wilds of New Jersey where they founded Princeton. Of course, it was equally bad for your health to be a Catholic in Dedham, or to be a Leveller, a Digger, or a Hutterite. In this detestable fashion Dedham was able to enjoy 234 years of religious purity before its Congregational monopoly was broken.

Well, what does this all mean? Just this: the negative side of local choice is very easy to see and even very easy to predict. We see it illustrated in the example of Colonial Dedham. But the whole matter is a good deal more complicated than assigning a bad grade to religious discrimination or to any other type of social choice that prescribes and limits a particular kind of human association. For instance, where could we begin to look for an explanation of how these people grew gradually more tolerant and came to accept all forms of religion? They even changed their conservative ways to the point where Massachusetts gained a national reputation as the most liberal state in the Union. That's quite a flip-flop to account for in the absence of compulsion, intimidation, or potent enabling legislation, isn't it. How did Dedham and the rest of those towns *teach themselves* to reform without experts making them do it and without central intervention? Remember, they only allowed the practitioners of one religion to vote. But they changed. And nobody forced them to do it. Something mysterious inside the structure of Congregationalism worked to have them abandon some of the exclusivity adherence to Biblical elite dogma had taught them.

I am certain that "something" was nearly unconditional local choice. It was self-correcting! Because the town churches did not team up to present an institutional orthodoxy that made each town just like another—as government monopoly schools do today—error in one church could be countered by its correction in another. As long as people had the choice to vote with their feet, the free market punished severe errors by leaving a congregation empty, just as it could reward a good place by filling it up. And even if enough rotten people were found to make a rotten town or rotten congregation, as long as there was no machinery in place for that one idea to compel all others to bow down before it, the human damage it could cause was strictly limited. Only when tools exist out of which a central orthodoxy can arise, like a pyramid, is there a real danger that some central poison can poison us all.

Yes, the negative aspects of local choice are easy to spot and the overwhelming argument in its favor—that without it the genius of democracy cannot exist—is hard to see. Because there is plenty of local tyranny too, the temptation is to cede power to a central authority in the name of fairness, to manage some best way for all from central headquarters. That's what a national curriculum is supposed to be for schools, a rational, fair way to legislate bad schooling out of existence. A national curriculum would never have allowed Dedham or Sudbury or Framingham or Wellfleet to develop as they did; that would have been dangerous, unpredictable, divisive—no, they would have been regulated centrally, as our schools are today, even without a national curriculum and national standards.

And here comes the dialectic. The experience of our centrally planned century has not been very good for most people. According to some, the planet itself is in jeopardy. And things legislated out of existence, like alcohol and drug abuse or racism, don't seem to go away—as religious exclusivity went away naturally in New England under a regime of local choice—instead, law appears to give bad habits an injection of virulent new life. Think of the great progressive victories won in the courts because social engineers were unable to build popular consensus, or were unwilling to wait: affirmative action, desegregation, graphic sexual imagery available at the local newsstand, various women's rights issues, and so on. Are these victories for the groups the courts sought to protect, or do these victories hold the same value they would have, had they been won through change in the social consensus? By most parameters the plight of Black Americans, for example, would seem to be worse than it was in 1960. Furthermore, a mean-spiritedness seems to exist everywhere, including our schools, that pours contempt and neglect on further efforts to give the descendants of slavery a hand. The predicament of women is a little trickier to see, but if sharply accelerated rates of suicide, heart disease, emotional illness, sterility, and other pathological conditions is an indicator, the admission of women *en masse* to the unisex workplace is not an unmixed blessing. Further, some disturbing evidence exists that the income of working *couples* in 1990 has only slightly more purchasing power than the income of the average working man did in 1910. In effect, two laborers are being purchased for the price of one—an outcome Adam Smith or David Ricardo might have predicted—and an unseen social cost has been the destruction of family life, the loss of home as sanctuary or haven, and the bewilderment of children raised by strangers from infancy.

Does central legal intimidation produce the social results it promises? Not so long ago narcotics were legal in the United States; while they were always a pernicious nuisance they never became an epidemic before legislation prohibiting their use came into existence. Is it possible that *compelling* people to do something guarantees that they will do it poorly, with a bad will, or indifferently, unless you are willing, as the Army is, to suspend most human rights and use any degree of intimidation necessary? And if the latter is the only way that compulsion can produce results, what is the *human* value of using it if it diminishes the quality of human life?

Multiple prohibitions of choice in the matter of education are now enforced by law, enshrining an exclusive bureaucracy of certified teachers and administrators, and literally hundreds of invisible agencies necessary to maintain the institution of government monopoly schooling. Defying the lessons of the market, this psychopathic megalith has grown more and more powerful in spite of colossal failures to educate throughout its history. It succeeds in surviving

only because it employs the police power of the
State to fill its hollow classrooms. It prohibits
local choice and variety and because of this
prohibition it has had a hideous effect on our
national moral fabric. The effect that the
national prohibition of alcohol by legislation
had on social cohesion and common values is
an object lesson too recent to forget, I hope. And
compared to the prohibitions that compulsory
government monopoly schooling imposes on
the children and families of a nation, alcohol
prohibition is a minor episode. By preventing
a free market in education, a handful of social
engineers—backed by the industries that profit
from compulsory schooling: teacher colleges,
textbook publishers, materials suppliers, et
al.—has ensured that most of our children will
not have an education, even though they may
be thoroughly schooled.

Divorced from religion, the congregational
principle is a psychological force propelling
individuals to reach their maximum potential
when working in small groups of people with
whom they feel in harmony. If you think about
this you wonder what purpose is achieved by
arranging things any other way. The Congregationalists understood profoundly that good
things happen to the human spirit *when it is
left alone.*

The best immediate evidence I have to offer
that leaving people alone to work out their own
local destinies is a splendid idea is the curious
sociology of my presence as a speaker in
Dedham last year. There, in a community that

had whipped half-naked Quaker women, stood I, a Roman Catholic, with a Scots Presbyterian wife, accompanied by my good friend Roland, half-pagan, half-Jewish, in a Unitarian church that had once been a Congregational parish. No act of the Massachusetts legislature made that possible, no pronouncement of the Supreme Court. People learned to be neighbors in Dedham because they were allowed real choice for three hundred years, including the choice to make their own mistakes. Everyone learned a better way to deal with difference than exclusion because they had time to think about it and work it through—time measured in generations.

But if they had been *ordered* to change, ordered as other immigrants were, to change their behavior and abandon their culture in compulsory schools set up for that purpose, I think what would have happened is this: some of them would have *seemed* to change but would have harbored such powerful resentments at being deprived of choice that some way to exact vengeance would have evolved. And most of the group deprived of choice and custom and family and roots would have reacted in a variety of ways to these social pressures, would have gone quietly insane or become simplified people, fit to haul stones to build someone else's pyramids, perhaps, or to watch television produce simplified fantasies, but fit for little else.

Despite the lip service we have continued to pay to local choice ever since congregational days, our schools are centrally planned and already have a national curriculum in place mediated by the textbook publishing industry and the standardized training of teachers. That our schools have failed spectacularly to give our children the education we want for them, or the selves we want, or to deliver on the dream of the democratic, classless society we still yearn for is obvious enough; what we miss is the logic of our failure. By allowing the imposition of direction from centers far beyond our control, we have time and again missed the lesson of the congregational principle: *that people are less than whole unless they gather themselves voluntarily* into groups of souls in harmony. Gathering themselves to pursue individual, family, and community dreams consistent with their private humanity is what makes them whole; only slaves are gathered by others. And these dreams must be written locally because to exercise any larger ambition without such a base is to lose touch with the things which give life meaning: self, family, friends, work, and intimate community.

There seem to me two "official" ways to look at the state of education in the United States these days, both of them wrong. First, we conceive it to be an engineering problem that can be made to yield to a pragmatic instrumental approach. From this vantage point there is a simple right and wrong way of schooling, never the thousand private individual possibilities the New England Congregationalists

might have believed. Second, we look upon
schooling is as if it were a character in a
continuous courtroom drama, a drama wherein
we search for the villains who have prevented
our kids from learning. Bad teachers, poor
textbooks, incompetent administrators, evil
politicians, ill-trained parents, bad children—
whomever the villains may be we shall find
them, indict them, arraign them, prosecute
them, perhaps even execute them! Then things
will be okay.

Out of these two wrong-headed ways of
looking at education have grown enormous
industries that claim power to cure mass-
education of its frictions or of its demons in
exchange for treasure. Into this carnival of
magical thinking has come a parade of profit-
seekers: analysts, consultants, researchers,
academic houses, writers, advisors, columnists,
textbook committees, school boards, testing
corporations, journalists, teachers' colleges,
state departments of education, monitors,
coordinators, manufacturers, certified teachers
and administrators, television programs, and
hordes of school-related businesses—all parasitic
growths of the government monopoly school
concept.

The greatest attraction of social engineering
and antisocial demonologies to many of us is
that both, at bottom, promise a quick fix. That
has always been the dark side of the American
dream, the search for an easy way out, a belief
in magic. The endless parade of promises that
constitutes the heart of American advertising,

one of the largest of our national enterprises, testifies to the deep well of superstition in our national foundation, which has been institutionalized in the advertising business. Easy money, easy health, easy beauty, easy education— if only the right incantation can be found. Lurking behind the magic is an image of people as machinery that can be built and repaired; this is our Calvinist legacy calling to us over the centuries, saying that the world and all its living variety is just machinery, not very hard to adjust if we put sentimentality aside and fire the villains, either symbolically or with actual bonfires, depending on the century. School reform to most of us is an engineer reaching for the right wrench or Perry Mason finding the clue he needs to nail the bad guy.

Ultimately, how we think about social problems depends on our philosophy of human nature: what we think people are, what we think they are capable of, what the purposes of human existence may be, if any. If people are machines then school can only be a way to make these machines more reliable; the logic of machines dictates that parts be uniform and interchangeable, all operations time-constrained, predictable, economical. Does this sound to you like the schools you attended, that your children attend? The Civil War unfortunately demonstrated beyond the shadow of a doubt both the financial and social utility of regimentation, but while this notion of people as machines has been around for thousands of years, its effective reign has only been operational since the end of World War I.

American education teaches by its methodology that people are machines. Bells ring, circuits open and close, energy flows or is constricted, qualities are reduced to a numbering system, a plan is followed of which the machine parts know nothing. Octavio Paz, the recent Nobel Prize winner from Mexico has this to say about our schools:

> In the North American system men and women are subjected from childhood to an inexorable process. Certain principles contained in brief formulas are endlessly repeated by the press, radio, television, churches and especially schools. A person imprisoned by these schemes is like a plant in a flowerpot too small for it. He cannot grow or mature. This sort of conspiracy cannot help but provoke violent individual rebellions.

We cannot grow or mature, like plants in too little flowerpots. We are addicted to dependency; in the current national crisis of maturity we seem to be waiting for the teacher to tell us what to do, but the teacher never comes to do that. Bridges collapse, men and women sleep on the streets, bankers cheat, good will decays, families betray each other, the government lies as a matter of policy, corruption, shame, sickness, and sensationalism are everywhere. No school has a curriculum to provide the quick fix.

The old Congregationalists would have been able to put their finger at once on the reason pyramidal societies, such as the one our monopoly form of schooling sustains, must always end in apathy and disorganization. At the root they are based on the lie that there is "one right way" in human affairs and that experts can be awarded the permanent direction of the enterprise of education. It is a lie because the changing dynamics of time and situation and locality render expertise irrelevant and obsolete shortly after it is anointed.

Monopoly schooling has been the chief training institution of the hive society. It certifies permanent experts who enjoy privileges of status unwarranted by the results they produce. Because these privileges, once achieved, will not willingly be given over, whole apparatuses of privilege have been fashioned that are impregnable to change. Even under the severest criticism they grow larger and more dangerous because they nourish important parts of our political and economic system. In the most literal sense they are impossible to reform because they have ceased to be human, having been transformed into abstract structures of superb efficiency, independent of lasting human control survival mechanisms. This is not a devil you can wrestle with as Daniel Webster did with Old Scratch, but one that has to be starved to death by depriving it of victims.

Monopoly schooling is the major cause of our loss of national and individual identity. It has institutionalized the division of social

classes and acted as an agent of caste—
repugnant to our founding myths and to the
reality of our founding period. Its strength
arises from many quarters, the antichild,
antifamily stream of history for one—but it
draws it greatest power from being a natural
adjunct to the kind of commercial economy we
have that requires permanently dissatisfied
consumers.

It's time to stop. This system doesn't work,
and it's one of the causes of our world coming
apart. No amount of tinkering will make the
school machine work to produce educated
people; education and schooling are, as we all
have experienced, mutually exclusive terms.
In 1930, sixty long years ago, Thomas Briggs,
delivering the Inglis Lecture at Harvard, charged
that "the nation's great investment in secondary
education has shown no respectable achievement"; two decades later, in 1951, a survey
made of 30,000 Los Angeles school children
discovered that seventy-five percent of eighth
graders couldn't find the Atlantic Ocean on a
map and most of them couldn't calculate
fifty percent of thirty-six. From my personal
experience, I stand witness that the situation
is certainly no better today.

What on earth is going on? Any genuine
debate would have to grapple with the uniform
failure of every type of government monopoly
school. With the addition of television, the
destructive power of schooling is now awesome
and thoroughly out of control. The television

institution, very similar to the structure of mass-schooling, has expanded so successfully that all the former escape routes are now blocked. We have destroyed the minds and characters of the nation's children by preempting their youth, removing their choices. We will pay a huge price in lost humanity for this crime for another century, even if a way is found to overturn the pyramid. Getting rid of the monopoly is the beginning of an answer.

What is there to do? Look to Dedham, to Sudbury, to Marblehead, and to Provincetown, all different yet all capable of meeting their community's needs. Turn your back on national solutions and toward communities of families as successful laboratories. Let us turn inward until we master the first directive of any philosophy worthy of the name, "Know Thyself." Understand that successful communities know the truth of the words "good fences make good neighbors," while at the same time are able to recognize, respect, understand, appreciate, and learn from each other's differences.

Look to the congregational principle for answers. Encourage and underwrite experimentation; trust children and families to know what is best for themselves; stop the segregation of children and the aged in walled compounds; involve everyone in the every community in the education of the young: businesses, institutions, old people, whole families; look for local solutions and always accept a personal solution in place of a corporate one. You need not fear educational consequences: reading, writing, and arithmetic aren't very hard to teach if you take pains to see that compulsion and the school agenda don't shortcircuit each individual's private appointment with themselves to learn these things. There is abundant evidence that less than a hundred hours is sufficient for a person to become totally literate and a self-teacher. Don't be panicked by scare tactics into surrendering your children to experts.

Teaching must, I think, be decertified as quickly as possible. That certified teaching experts like myself are deemed necessary to make learning happen is a fraud and a scam. Look around you: the results of teacher-college licensing are in the schools you see. Let anybody who wants to, teach; give families back their tax money to pick and choose—who could possibly be a better shopper if the means for comparison were made available? Restore the congregation system by encouraging competition after a truly unmanipulated free-market model— in that way the social dialectic can come back to life. Trust in families and neighborhoods and individuals to make sense of the important question, "What is education *for*? If some of them answer differently than you might prefer, that's really not your business, and it shouldn't be your problem. Our type of schooling has deliberately concealed that such a question *must* be framed and not taken for granted if anything beyond a mockery of democracy is to be nurtured. It is illegitimate to have an expert answer that question for you. It was our trust in our potential that helped lay down our

foundations back in the colonial period, and I feel certain that the structure we built still houses powerful potential. Let's use it, and create a truly American solution to the great school nightmare.